The New Labour Experiment

THE NEW LABOUR EXPERIMENT

Change and Reform
Under Blair and Brown

FLORENCE FAUCHER-KING
PATRICK LE GALÈS

Translated by Gregory Elliott

FOREWORD BY JONAH LEVY

STANFORD UNIVERSITY PRESS

Stanford, California

Stanford University Press
Stanford, California
English translation © 2010 by the Board of Trustees of the
Leland Stanford Junior University

The New Labour Experiment: Change and Reform Under Blair and
Brown was originally published in French in 2007 under the title
Tony Blair 1997–2007: Le bilan des réformes © 2007 Presses de la
Fondation nationale des sciences politiques.

Library of Congress Cataloging-in-Publication Data

Faucher-King, Florence.
  [Tony Blair, 1997–2007. English]
  The New Labour experiment : change and reform under Blair and
Brown / Florence Faucher-King and Patrick Le Galès ; foreword by
Jonah Levy.
    p. cm.
  Revised, updated translation of: Tony Blair, 1997–2007. [Paris] :
Presses de la Fondation nationale des sciences politiques, c2007.
  Includes bibliographical references.
  ISBN 978-0-8047-6234-2 (cloth : alk. paper) —
  ISBN 978-0-8047-6235-9 (pbk. : alk. paper)
  1. Labour Party (Great Britain). 2. Blair, Tony, 1953–.
3. Brown, Gordon, 1951– . 4. Great Britain—Politics and
government—1997–2007. 5. Great Britain—Politics and
government—2007–. I. Le Galès, Patrick. II. Title.
JN1129.L32F3513 2010
324.2410709'.0511—dc22

                                          2009046620

Printed in the United States of America on acid-free, archival-
quality paper

Typeset at Stanford University Press in 10.5/15 Minion

Thank you to Lila for bringing fun, play, and sunshine into my life—Florence

To Robin and Tiphaine—Patrick

Contents

Acknowledgment   ix

Note to Readers   x

Foreword by Jonah Levy   xi

Introduction   1

1. The British Business Model versus the European Social Model   17

   The Activist, Innovative State, 18   The Resumption of Public
   Investment, 22   A Long-term Project, 24   Improving
   Competitiveness, 26   Incentives and Coercion on the Labor Market, 29
   Social-Democratic Options?, 32   The Issue of Inequalities, 35
   Uneven Achievements, 38

2. Bureaucratic Revolution, or Privatization of Public Services?   42

   Transformation of Public Action and the State Apparatus: The Thatcher
   Revolution, 44   Think Tanks and the New Labour Elites, 47   "Activist"
   Governments, 49   Control through Information, 54   Auditing Society, 59

3. Decentralizing or Centralizing Institutions?   62

   Polycentric and Asymmetrical Governance, 64   Constitutional Reform:
   Tinkering in Progress, 71   The "Europeanization" of British Politics?, 76
   Centralization of the Executive, 80   Communications and Rationalization
   of the Executive, 83

4. The Reinvention of the Labour Party. "New Labour,
   New Britain"   88

   Loosening the Links with the Trade Unions, 90   Promoting a Direct
   Relationship with Members, 93   A "Managed" and Disciplined Party, 96

A Search for Effective and Professional Funding, 98   The Party as
Communications Enterprise, 100   Discussion and Control of the Policy
Agenda, 101   New Labour's Media Offensive, 104

5. Democratization or Control?   110
The Citizen-Consumer, 111   Virtual Engagement and Real Funding, 115
Participatory Democracy, Democratic Illusion, 119   The Return of
Protest, 122   Order and Security: "Cruel Britannia," 124

Conclusion: Toward a Market Society   133

Postscript: The Fall of New Labour   143
Devolution: From British Politics to National Arenas, 147   New Labour
and the Global Economic Crisis, 149   The Party: What Happens to
New Labour ?, 152   From Crises to Disaster, Catastrophe,
and Debacle, 155

Notes   159

Bibliography   175

Acknowledgment

The authors wish to thank Presses de Sciences Po for making this translation possible.

Note to Readers

This book on the New Labour decade was first written in the final year of the Blair government and originally published the day that Tony Blair stepped out of Number 10 Downing Street, leaving the leadership of his party and the country to Gordon Brown. In the years since Blair's departure, we have revisited and revised this book to bring it up to date concerning the (d)evolution of New Labour under Brown. While the book's core chapters refer to the decade in which Tony Blair presided as Prime Minister and Gordon Brown as Chancellor of the Exchequer, we have concluded the book with an assessment of the Brown government to date.

Foreword by Jonah Levy

Florence Faucher-King and Patrick Le Galès have crafted an incisive, readable analysis of the Blair-Brown years in Britain. The book is neither a detailed policy study nor a grand theoretical treatise. Rather, it is an analytical essay, theoretically informed, that paints the broad brushstrokes of New Labour's decade in power, while grappling with its larger meaning. The book focuses primarily on domestic policy and governance; issues of foreign policy, such as Tony Blair's relationship with George Bush and the decision to go to war in Iraq, figure less prominently. The book's greatest strength lies in drawing out the implications for left-wing parties that are seeking to adapt to a world of neoliberal globalization—in particular, the implications for policy, governance, and party organization.

New Labour has pursued two main goals. The first is to improve social justice in what is essentially a neoliberal economic order without disturbing the mechanisms that allow that order to function. Alongside this economic objective, New Labour has pursued a second, more political or electoral objective. Here, the goal has been to transform the Labour Party into a cross-class party, able to appeal beyond its shrinking working-class ghetto to Britain's middle class.

These goals are not all that different from those of the Democratic Party in the United States under Bill Clinton or Barack Obama. What is different, however, are the means deployed by New Labour. Faucher-King and Le Galès describe how Blair and Brown have made aggressive use of state power. As French academics, Faucher-King and Le Galès know of what they speak. But whereas state authorities in France have generally endeavored to steer or direct the market, New Labour has sought to bend the population to the logic of the market, to create a "market society," as the authors describe it, borrowing from Karl Polanyi.

New Labour's statist approach has multiple origins. Scholars have long noted that Britain's political system—with its cabinet government, first-past-the-post electoral law, unwritten constitution, and limited judicial review—gives the prime minister tremendous capacity to pursue his or her ambitions. But Faucher-King and Le Galès point to two more intriguing reasons for New Labour's statism.

The first is the obsession with avoiding a repeat of Labour's last governing experience in the late 1970s. The Callaghan government was unhinged and the door to Margaret Thatcher opened, not only by poor economic management but also by a perceived inability to govern, to stand up to the trade unions, as crystallized in the unrest of the so-called Winter of Discontent (1978–79). Labour then spent eighteen years in helpless opposition, as Thatcher and John Major moved the country in a sharply neoliberal direction, in no small part the result of the party's internal divisions and ideological posturing. For Blair and Brown, then, showing that New Labour is competent to govern means projecting a unified message and controlling the rank and file. Order is to be preferred over spontaneity and feedback.

The second reason for New Labour's statism, as highlighted by Faucher-King and Le Galès, is intellectual as opposed to historical. Blair and Brown have displayed a tremendous faith in social engineering. The state, using all manner of audits and quantitative evaluations, can tightly manage complex organizations, such as the National Health Service (NHS). It can also deploy carrots and sticks to "incentivize" individuals to behave in a socially desirable manner, to take up jobs instead of crime. Although New Labour is often portrayed as continuing or tinkering with the Thatcher legacy, Faucher-King and Le Galès show that, in fact, it has been pursuing a highly ambitious, activist agenda.

How has this activist agenda fared? In the economic and social arena, Faucher-King and Le Galès indicate that the record looked reasonably good (albeit with a number of caveats). Blair and Brown presided over a decade of strong growth, low unemployment, and sound public finances. While reassuring business and financial interests, the government managed to find resources for an array of antipoverty programs, primarily tax credits for working families, that helped to reduce poverty significantly. The government was also able to make massive investments in long-neglected public services, most notably education and health care.

Statist social engineering played a critical role in legitimating this increased public spending. Antipoverty programs were targeted at working families: pressure was intensified on the unemployed to take jobs, and those who remained outside the workforce often saw their benefits reduced. Reflecting an almost Victorian ethic, the British state would reward work, while punishing indolence (or incapacity). In deference to middle-class values of frugality, the state would also ensure that money was well spent: increased funding for health and education was coupled with the "new public management" methods inaugurated by the Conservatives. Whether practices—such as the separation of purchasers from providers, so-called public-private partnerships, Private Finance Initiatives (PFIs), and a multitude of audits and quantitative performance indicators—actually improved the quality and efficiency of public services is a matter of considerable dispute. What is beyond dispute, however, is that these practices provided political cover to a New Labour government that was spending a lot of money on Old Labour priorities, from fighting poverty to improving health care and education.

Of course, the financial meltdown has taken the shine off many of New Labour's economic and social achievements. But the criticisms of New Labour go beyond money. Faucher-King and Le Galès show that Blair's and Brown's statist approach has taken a toll on democracy and civil liberties, both across the country and within the Labour Party itself.

New Labour came to power on a pledge to revitalize British freedoms and pluralism after eighteen years of Conservative authoritarian, centralizing rule. Faucher-King and Le Galès note that the initial years of the Blair government saw some important reforms, such as the ratification of the European Convention on Human Rights, the creation of elected assemblies in Scotland, Wales, and Northern Ireland, and the re-establishment of an elected government for the greater London area. These reforms were largely one-shot deals, however. Devolution remained a kind of half-hearted institutional bricolage, rather than far-reaching reform, which failed to alter Britain's position as the most centralized political system in Europe.

New Labour's record on civil liberties is even more disappointing, according to Faucher-King and Le Galès. In the wake of 9/11, the government passed three laws strengthening police powers, including the right to detain foreign suspects indefinitely without charge. Even before 9/11, New Labour had been extremely aggressive in combating crime so as to neutralize this potential Conservative wedge issue and reassure the fearful middle classes. Incarceration, already high by European standards, increased by nearly 20 percent under Blair; computerized ID cards were introduced without any kind of safeguards; antisocial behavior, such as public drunkenness or lack of respect for a police officer, was made into criminal offenses; and camera surveillance in public spaces was expanded to the point where the average British subject is photographed three hundred times a day.

The same centralizing tendencies and concern for reassuring the middle classes have refashioned the internal workings of the Labour Party. Faucher-King and Le Galès describe four main changes introduced by Blair. First, the power of the unions was curtailed; indeed, the government often portrayed itself as at odds with the unions, so as to appear "modern" and committed to the general interest as opposed to narrow pressure groups. Second, the party shifted from a workerist orientation to a middle-class orientation, perhaps best symbolized by the substitution of the word "colleague" for "comrade" at party meetings. Third, the party became extremely centralized, limiting input from militants and unions, tightly controlling debate at party congresses, and keeping all representatives "on message" in their public utterances. Fourth, the party diversified and expanded its fund-raising, moving from almost complete dependence on the unions to massive fund-raising from private sources. The result of these changes, according to Faucher-King and Le Galès, has been a party that is tightly disciplined, professional, polished, and well funded. New Labour has become a formidable electoral machine and a steadfast pillar of the government.

On the downside, the top-down control has demoralized and demobilized loyal members; the constant "spin" of Labour leaders has bred cynicism and distrust among the public; private fund-raising has led to a number of corruption scandals; and the party has lost its links to both new ideas and social movements.

Among U.S. observers, particularly Democrats, the British political system can inspire a certain degree of envy. Like Tony Blair, Barack Obama wants to modernize and moralize a liberal political economy, while building a coalition between the disadvantaged and the middle class. But unlike Blair, Obama has to deal with Blue Dog Democrats and Senate filibusters. Imagine what Obama could accomplish if he headed a parliamentary system and unitary state. National health insurance, effective financial regulation, and more just fiscal policies would all be within reach! Faucher-King's and Le Galès's penetrating analysis of the Blair years offers a cautionary tale, however. Whatever economic and social gains Blair and Brown may have achieved, and those remain subject to both dispute and potential reversal, they have come at a very high political price. As Faucher-King and Le Galès demonstrate, a young, charismatic, center-left leader with fresh ideas and the power to pursue them can be a decidedly mixed blessing.

Introduction

May 1997: The mildness of a beautiful spring day makes the excitement gripping Britain palpable. After eighteen years of Conservative government—twelve of them under the Iron Lady, Margaret Thatcher—the British are about to vote for the Labour Party, or rather New Labour. The suspense is short-lived; a landslide gives the young leader Tony Blair and his team a massive majority. The euphoria lasts late into the night and everyone is hoping for the advent of the "cool Britannia" promised by the new prime minister.

May 2007: The heroes are weary. The Blair government is suffering the consequences of the war in Iraq, while criticisms abound, provoked by the crisis of the National Heath Service and the authoritarian drift that is transforming the country into "cruel Britannia." The party that claimed to restore honesty in politics is reeling from a police investigation into a case of corruption involving New Labour's leaders and Tony Blair's closest colleagues. Already weakened by the announcement of his departure in the course of his third term, the prime minister, in September 2006, has been forced to announce his retirement early the next year. He has thus lost much of his authority. With Blair's departure in June 2007, the hour has come for balance sheets.

For ten years, the New Labour governments represented a genuine project of social change and demonstrated an exceptional capacity for implementing reforms. Given the electoral system in Britain (majoritarian, with a single round in one-member constituencies), the winning party can usually count on an absolute majority in the House of Commons, which allows it, with the support of about one-third of the electorate, to form a strong, stable government. The activism of the New Labour governments cannot be understood without taking into account the sizable majorities obtained in 1997 and 2001. The party, which had never proved capable of retaining power for two consecutive terms, won three successive electoral victories, guaranteeing it a supremacy in Parliament (in the House of Commons) superior to that ever obtained by the Conservatives. Their scale insulated the Blair governments against internal rebellions or attacks from the opposition. Furthermore, New Labour benefited from the ongoing weakness of the Conservative Party, which was ideologically divided, lacking a large parliamentary cohort—it was reduced to a parliamentary group of 167 MPs (members of Parliament), the lowest since 1907—and incapable for many years of effectively performing its role of opposition.

The "Blair decade" gives us a significant retrospect to analyze the actions and some of the results of the New Labour governments. A new government always announces numerous reforms, a radical change in a short space of time. Observers scrutinize the actions of ministers and MPs; they emphasize the role of courageous, visionary governments. They reveal the stage-managing of "decisions" that create historic moments that are supposed to change the course of public policy. This heroic version almost invariably derives from an illusion, a spotlight focused on a particular moment in a longer, more complicated process; on a man or woman caught up in careers, networks, interests, and institutions.

Public policies change less readily than slogans. Innovations are often assemblages of existing programs, sometimes disguised by new names. Change in public policy is often incremental,[1] because any new government inherits a civil service, a budget, and institutions that constrain its actions. Although, after eighteen years of opposition, Labour was impatient to demonstrate its capacity for change, analysis of the legacy is indispensable to assess the profundity of the changes made.

The disputed balance sheet of the Labour governments is generally subject to three rather contrasting interpretations (Hassan, 2007); we shall sug-

TABLE 1

Results of Elections to the House of Commons

Year	Turnout (%)	Labour vote (%)	Labour MPs seats (no.)	Labour MPs seats (%)	Difference*
1997	71.3	44	418	63.6	178
2001	59.4	40.7	412	62.5	166
2005	61.4	35.2	355	55	66

*Difference between the number of Labour seats and those of the Opposition.

gest a fourth.[2] The first interpretation stresses the reformist work of the Blair governments, in continuity with the reforms undertaken during the two major periods of Labour government—that is, the Attlee governments (1945–51), marked by the creation of the National Health Service; and the Wilson governments (1964–70, and then 1974–76, although Jim Callaghan remained Labour prime minister until 1979). Continuing the Labour tradition, the Blair governments modernized the party and the country by pursuing Labour's traditional goals: economic growth, job support, redistribution, investment in public services, and, more generally, pursuit of a progressive political agenda as regards morals and the protection of minorities. Labour, which from the outset was reformist, has always had ambiguous relations with employers, the City of London,[3] the establishment, and the economy. Its reforming zeal often encountered difficulties that can be explained in part by its relationship to the state,[4] the monarchy and its institutions, and the absence of a revolutionary tradition. In addition, others stress that the closing stages of Labour governments have always terminated in bitter criticisms from the left, an exodus of activists from the party, a very mixed record, long periods in opposition . . . and, a few decades later, rehabilitation of the reformist record (Gamble, 2007).

By contrast, a second interpretation casts Tony Blair and his governments as gravediggers of the Labour Party, consolidators of the results of Thatcherism, and the most rabid defenders of market mechanisms. After 1994, Tony Blair renamed his party and imposed a redefinition of collective objectives.[5] Following Thatcher, the Blair governments strengthened the strong state and the market economy[6]—that is, the mobilization of the resources of a centralized, sometimes authoritarian state in order to reform, to strengthen the logic of competition and create a British *homo economicus*, rational, egoistic, competitive, and adapted to the implacable logic of the globalized economy. On the other hand, they abandoned any strong discourse on equality, the role of the public sector, or social-democracy.

A third reading, favored by the actors themselves, alludes to a "Third Way"—an alternative to the modus operandi of both Old Labour and the Conservatives. This interpretation of the New Labour revolution stresses the modernization of the means but not the goals of the British left, insisting on the originality and significance of the reforms and the unprecedented electoral success of the Blair governments. It highlights the original doctrine of the Third Way, theorized by the British sociologist Anthony Giddens: it rejects socialism and capitalism and insists on novel constraints on public action in a world dominated by the logics of globalization and technological revolution, the advent of the knowledge society. Blair's "way" is said to derive from new work on governance that goes beyond hierarchies and the traditional civil service (Rhodes, 1996; Le Galès, 2006)—that is, the role of networks, partnerships, cooperatives, new tools of public action, as well as the doctrine of communitarianism (Bevir, 2005). New Labour presented themselves as pragmatists, radical centrists concerned with the efficiency of public action, haunted by the constant requirement to modernize Britain so as to meet the challenges of globalization. This interpretation, rooted in ideas, has been somewhat sidelined: since 2001, New Labour has abandoned any reference to the Third Way.

In this work, we propose a fourth interpretation that insists on the composite and original character of the model. It is based not on the ideology of Tony Blair and his teams, but on their actions, on the policies that have been implemented and on their impact on British politics and society. A decade is a long time in politics, making it possible to perceive inflexions and dynamics. We seek to clarify the contours of the New Labour project, deemed complex by commentators, and to dispel the perplexity created by the activism of the Blair governments (Lewis, 2003). New Labour is indeed a hybrid of economic liberalism inspired by American reforms, the legacy of English-style social-democracy, illiberal policies in the political sense (that is, those that coerce individuals), and openness or democratization, the whole being seasoned by a marked taste for experimentation.

Three points, which will be at the center of this work, seem essential to us for the purposes of drawing up this balance sheet.

(1) An inscription in history and a desire to transform, to act on British society.

The New Labour elites are profoundly marked by history. They want to be modernizers who are going to adapt the country to a new "historical phase" ("new times") marked by globalization. New Labour thus displays a rather linear conception of history, of which they are also the agents. Changes are regarded as ineluctable. What is at stake is seizing, even anticipating, the opportunities for development that they create, in order to possess influence on the international stage and master economic constraints. The systematic program for "modernizing" Britain, be it the party, the state, the economy, or society, has been developed without any qualms, because it was presented as a response to the inexorable globalization of the economy. As Anthony Giddens has written, "[T]he world doesn't owe us anything."

Modernization is a portmanteau word, which for New Labour is at once an imperative, an aspiration, an injunction, and a description of their political actions (Finlayson, 2003). They are not content to accept the Thatcherite inheritance; they regard economic globalization and the need for sound economic management as a fait accompli. It is necessary to adapt to a world that is changing ineluctably and irremediably. Lack of change is synonymous with regression. Only modernization, defended by Blair in messianic tones,[7] makes it possible to maintain a competitive advantage in a knowledge economy. Its content is rather vague, but it generally involves the use of new technologies, the need for permanent training throughout life and flexibility in the job market and individual careers, the adoption of managerial modes from the private sector, and privileging competition and individual incentives. In speeches, public policy, and public relations, the invocation of modernization becomes the open sesame that simultaneously differentiates and identifies. It allowed Tony Blair to denounce the forces of conservatism in the Labour Party (those who accept neither the organizational changes nor the new policy directions), and in the country (those who want to preserve their privileges and thereby prevent the opening up of multiple opportunities to deserving individuals), without really justifying the concrete content of his proposals.

Taking account of history ultimately translates into accepting the Conservative legacy and the failures of the Labour Party. The New Labourites retain a bitter memory of the economic difficulties of previous Labour governments, especially those of Wilson and Callaghan. In the 1970s, Britain experienced a profound crisis. It was regarded as the sick man of Europe. The appeal to the International Monetary Fund in 1976, during an unprecedented financial crisis, or the countless strikes culminating in the "Winter of Discontent" of 1978–79, served as a brutal indication of the decline that the country was undergoing.[8] These failures made the Conservative victory possible.

While the project pursued by Margaret Thatcher aroused no enthusiasm, alternative solutions failed. The Conservative governments offered the British a way out of crisis based on the idea of the superiority of market mechanisms to a contested public sector that was performing poorly. The appeal to return to the model of a less interventionist but more efficient state, to the dynamism and effort of individuals and families at the expense of public-sector trade unions and bureaucracy, to the restoration of British greatness, resonated with the population. The Thatcher governments combined a strong ideological orientation with tactical and pragmatic implementation. They created new tools for developing a more centralized government. New Labour inherited a Britain that had been profoundly transformed, especially by privatization. Any return to the past was impossible. For Labour to get back into power, the public had to be persuaded that the party had changed; and to do that, the activists had to be persuaded to change.

(2) A mobilization of the state in the direction of a bureaucratic revolution that prioritizes the relationship between state, individual (consumer-citizens), and communities at the expense of intermediate organizations and bodies. Political activity organized around the desire to persuade, to win over.

Tony Blair and his teams reinforced an original conception of the state, different from the social-democratic version that privileges public-sector intervention, universal benefits, and close relations with trade unions. Even so, they were not supporters of a neoliberalism aiming for a retreat of the state. Quite the reverse, they mobilized the state to carry out reforms and change behavior. The Blair governments were extraordinarily active, even activist. They succeeded in introducing a remarkable number of reforms despite opposition and resistance. Blair and his ministers took risks. They engaged tirelessly, in order to explain, to justify, to arrive at compromises, to make assessments. Public policy involves choosing clienteles and victims. Tony Blair and his team never concealed the extent of the pressure that the state must exert in order to transform society, nor the importance of "difficult choices." Blair did not defend an enchanted vision of the world involving governance without coercion; he demonstrated a remarkable ability to mobilize resources and props for incessant reform. But such activism did not prevent some bitter setbacks. Ultimately, the ambition of social engineering to improve society, and reliance on the best research in the social sciences (especially economics) and on empirically proven facts, recall Nordic social-democracy.[9] Taking account of experts and stakeholders (those with a "stake" in the affair) was supposed not only to indicate what people want but also to suggest the technical measures to be taken to respond to their demands.

The reform program was carried out by mobilizing and developing the government's capacity for control and leadership. Preserving and adapting the framework bequeathed by the Conservatives, modernizing the utilitarian legacy (no trust in society), New Labour systematically reformed government and the ways in which it operates. The Blair governments massively increased the centralization of Britain, by granting more autonomy to individuals and organizations within a system of strengthened constraints and controls—a sophisticated system of what Michel Foucault would have called "conducting conduct"—which is not always free of a bureaucratic, even authoritarian drift. Is modernization tantamount to centralization?

"Political modernization" in fact resulted in the exclusion of institutions and groups in favor of communications professionals and a politics focused on image—an example of "post democracy" (Crouch, 2004). The constant concern for public relations, the professionalization of the government's and the party's political communications, led observers to question media hype and publicity maneuvers and query the substance of government policies. Thus, it is sometimes difficult to distinguish reality from its media projection—that is, from spin.[10]

The Blair governments generalized analytical models derived from rational choice theory and neoclassical economics,[11] introducing market mechanisms, developing incentives and penalties in order to alter the behavior of individuals and transform them into consumers of services maximizing their interests. They relied on local communities, parent associations, or religious groups—and no longer on traditional working-class activist networks. New Labour promoted an original model of political liberalism that has resulted in progressive reforms for integrating minorities and women's rights. At the same time, however, political participation has been discouraged, or rather (to adopt Paul Hirst's phrase), efforts have been directed to "maximizing minimum participation."[12]

In a context marked by a new terrorist threat, political liberalism, social-democracy and neoliberalism form a strange hybrid, object of controversies over the assessment of reforms

(3) A societal project for the middle classes, organized around work, winners, and consumption.

The Labour Party has always been led by an alliance between trade unionists and elites derived from the world of labor on the one hand, and bourgeois elites who have passed through Oxford or Cambridge on the other. We find this characteristic among the New Labour elites, which comprise former workers or trade unionists like John Prescott, MP for Hull in north-east England, or Alan Johnson. However, the new Blairite elites no longer possessed any nostalgia for the labor movement; nor were they obsessed with improving the quality of life of the least well off groups. They represented the middle and upper classes and aspired to educational excellence and individual and material success. Meritocracy was counterposed to the old Conservative elites. New Labour adopted a vision that values winners, entrepreneurs (whatever their color, background, or age), and security of property and persons; the issues of integration into society and redistribution or discourse on solidarity and public space were set aside.

This is also explained by the political strategy of realignment adopted by New Labour to make the party electable. Thatcher had driven the party back into its historical bastions: the north, Scotland, Wales, London, and big towns and cities. To win power and keep it, New Labour needed to win constituencies in the Midlands, the south, and the south-west, controlled by the middle classes: hence the importance of the themes of public services, competition, taxes, and security. New Labour's political strategy of realignment was based on winning over "Middle England"—a rosy representation of the middle and upper classes living in their own houses in the small towns of a verdant England. Tony Blair constantly wooed them with a view to conquering the center ground and driving the Conservatives to the right. He is himself a good representative of the progressive, meritocratic bourgeoisie. His modernizing language, with its moralistic accents, succeeded in convincing the middle classes of the importance of better public services. His wife is a successful lawyer; they have four children (the last of them born in 2000); and he knew how to combine the demands of family life and working life. The Blairs had the way of life of cosmopolitan upper-middle classes, breaking with traditional Labour. They spent their holidays in Tuscany or on a Caribbean island, in the villas of rich and famous friends, rock stars, or businessmen. By contrast, Blair was not always at ease with the trade unions, representatives of the towns of northern England, the Scottish, or Welsh—traditional pillars of the party.

These three dimensions of the New Labour project evolved over the course of ten years. The dynamism created by the phase of winning power was gradually institutionalized, becoming what was sometimes regarded as a quest for change for its own sake. Returning to the Blair era and New Labourism should not lead us to forget the existence of periods whose limits are not strictly defined. In the first phase, attempts at modernization focused primarily on the party's organization and its image, while projects for social reform were barely developed. The first term was marked by a determination to assert the credibility of the new Labour Party as economic manager, public services reformer, and European actor. Never before had the Labour Party succeeded in staying in government for two terms. Constrained in their early years by the promise to govern within the financial framework determined by the Conservatives, it was only with the second crushing victory of 2001 that the New Labour governments were able to invest massively in public services and accelerate reform of them. The economic growth that allowed Gordon Brown to establish his authority as a triumphant chancellor was based not only on prudent management but also on a favorable global context. The third term was marked by the domestic political consequences of the controversial commitment of British troops to Iraq. The reforms were pursued, but they had lost their novelty and now seemed ideological.

Finally, the government's dynamic was marked by the association and rivalry between two political leaders who dominated their generation in Britain, Tony Blair and Gordon Brown. Young MPs first elected in 1983, they were then around thirty years old (Brown is three years older) and shared an office in Parliament. They formed an alliance to conquer the party in 1994. Legend has it that, during dinner in a restaurant in Islington (flagship area for the embourgeoisement of north London), Gordon Brown agreed not to run against Tony Blair in the leadership contest.[13] In exchange, he is said to have promised to hand Gordon Brown complete control over planning of the manifesto and the economy, as well as his succession . . . one day. Appointed chancellor of the exchequer (finance and economics minister), Gordon Brown made the Treasury the control center and cockpit of government action. While Blair's strength was media savvy and his political geniality, Brown excelled at strategic organization. Thus was formed a strange tandem—a duo of hostile brothers. The two men constructed their teams, their base in the party and in the parliamentary majority. Their growing rivalry partially blocked the reformist dynamic and poisoned the Labour Party.[14] One cannot understand the development and tensions within New Labour without taking into account two of its main architects and their intersecting careers (see pages 12–13).

Tony Blair had discovered an international role during the intervention in Kosovo and the negotiations in Ireland. Subsequently, he appealed to people to grasp every opportunity to advance the values of Western democracy and human rights in the world. He engaged in the war against Iraq in good faith, mobilizing all the resources of his political skills and the state apparatus to persuade his fellow citizens, his party, and the press. The intervention was accepted under protest, and Tony Blair's political credit was irreparably damaged when evidence emerged of the manipulation of information (reinforced by the suicide of a scientist), and the conflict between Blair's advisers and the media turned into a confrontation (along with the departure of the chairman of the BBC, the British Broadcasting Corporation). The fact that British troops got bogged down in Iraq and were associated with abuses clouded the picture still further. The left has never forgiven him. Demonstrations by the war's opponents were the largest in the last thirty years. Caricatured as a liar and manipulator, Blair lost the trust of a significant segment of the British population. When the Labour Party risked electoral defeat in 2005, he owed his victory in extremis to the prioritization of Gordon Brown's economic record. Although that played a crucial role in explaining how Tony Blair lost his magic touch with the electorate and became an electoral liability for the party,[15] we have left to one side the issue of Iraq and chosen instead to concentrate on the internal reforms conducted in the country during the decade of Blair's premiership.

The debate on the balance sheet is all the more lively in that the story is not over. Gordon Brown, unstained chancellor of the exchequer and chief architect of the New Labour reforms, is Tony Blair's successor. At the end of June 2007 he inherited a party beset by doubt, weary after ten years in power, and divided over its project.

The government's actions and the reforms are not a matter of indifference across the Channel. Reference to Blair's reforms was a recurrent feature of the French presidential campaign in 2007. In 1997 the Jospin government had taken care to cultivate its difference, and the French Socialist Party had opposed the Third Way invoked by both Blair and Schröder. In 2007, for the left and the extreme left, Blair remained the symbol of the detested "liberal socialism," the friend of the bosses who support globalization. However, others, particularly in foundations with close links to English think tanks, lauded Blairism. The French Socialist Party did not

Tony Blair and Gordon Brown:
Two Leaders in Charge of the New Labour Governments

Tony Blair

Educated in a prestigious private school and then at Oxford, he became member of Parliament for Sedgefield (north-east England) in 1983. He is unquestionably the political leader—an indefatigable debater in Parliament and the media alike—capable of putting changes into perspective and an outstanding speaker. A young barrister, he has a marvelous touch with the media thanks to his gift for a phrase. He knows how to destabilize his opponents and demonstrates political courage on issues that seem to him to be essential. His talents make him a formidable machine for winning elections, but his relations with the Labour Party are difficult.[16] Tony Blair does not present himself as a man of the left, but as a progressive, a centrist who has pushed the Conservatives to the right: radical in his desire to modernize Britain but pragmatic as regards the means to be employed.

First leader of the baby-boom generation, he warmly embraces the theses of economic globalization.

He is in favor of immigration, openness, globalization, and the European Union.

He has the zeal of a preacher and a vision of the future that he wants to develop not only in Britain but also internationally. He supports causes. He wants to go beyond ideologies in order to create a just society that takes account of the constraints of globalization, the knowledge economy, and the new technology economy. He is ambitious for everyone and never tires of persuading and converting. "What will he do on the seventh day?" commentators worried, after a speech in 2001 in which he set out his ambitious projects for reform in all directions: poverty, terrorism, the environment, and so on. He displays his religious beliefs more openly than British political leaders traditionally do. He plays on the image of the accessible, sincere, honest, direct, and pragmatic human being.

He claims to be seeking to establish a direct relationship with voters, to want to liberate individuals from forms of conservatism so that they can fully develop their potential and choose their own way in life.

Tony Blair relied on a considerable team, composed in particular of convinced reformers like Peter Mandelson—grandson of the Labour leader Herbert Morrison—and Roger Liddle from the Social Democratic Party; intellectuals like John Gray and Anthony Giddens; communications advisors with a detailed knowledge of public opinion and the media like Philip Gould and Alastair Campbell. He also surrounded himself with a generation of politicians who were to have more or less successful ministerial careers, such as Patricia Hewitt, Charles Clarke, John Reid, Alan Milburn, Stephen Byers, Ruth Kelly, David Miliband, and advisors gravitating around think tanks or public relations firms. Upon leaving Downing Street,

Tony Blair became the international envoy of the United States and the European Union with the mission of promoting peace in the Middle East. Paradoxically, he seemed unaware that his role in the second war in Iraq made him an unlikely negotiation broker in the region. Having converted to Catholicism, he also joined Yale University as the Howland Distinguished Fellow in 2008, where he lectured on "faith and globalization."

Gordon Brown

This son of a Presbyterian minister has been member of Parliament for Dunfermline East since 1983. A former student leader, he is the author of a history thesis and an academic. He soon became a professional politician in the Scottish Labour movement (trade unions and party) and is a former chairman of the Scottish Labour Party. He has a reputation for being a rigorous but dour intellectual, for being prudent, for having an exceptional capacity for work, and for demanding as much of his colleagues. He prioritizes long-term strategies. Distrustful of Europe, he is an admirer of the United States but also of Sweden. Although an excellent speaker and debater, he does not have Blair's natural fluency with the media.

More at ease with traditional supporters of the party than Tony Blair, he has always cultivated his relations with the unions. He is more rooted in the Labour tradition of modernization and close to social-democracy but is also a convert to rational choice approaches. Nevertheless, Brown has less confidence than Blair in market mechanisms for redistributing or organizing certain services, such as heath care or education. On the other hand, he is intransigent on the elimination of restrictions liable to limit the competitiveness of firms in terms of regulation— for example, in the labor market. He has invested a lot in the reorganization of the state and the machinery of government.

Like Blair, Brown is surrounded by a team of highly organized advisors, brilliant young men (including Ed Balls, his economics advisor; Ed Miliband; and Charles Wheelan, his media spokesman) who come from the same backgrounds but are in touch with more traditional Labour networks. Blair left Brown to handle the details of government action, the tools, and the finances. Gradually Brown took control of the machinery of government, to the point of regularly being in a position to block the prime minister's projects, for example on adopting the euro or the role of the private sector in hospitals. In return Blair often sought to reduce the influence of his chancellor and the ministers close to him (Nick Brown, Douglas Alexander, Alistair Darling), without ever wishing to dispense with them.

Gradually, Brown became the government's strong man, key strategist in the electoral campaigns of 2001 and 2005. Contained in the role of grand vizier longer than he had hoped, champing at the bit while not daring to be utterly disloyal, Brown ended up securing (forcing?) Blair's public commitment to retire in 2007. On 27 June 2007, he replaced him as leader of the Labour Party and prime minister.

really know what to make of this experience, whose electoral and economic success has been impressive. While the party remained massively hostile, the presidential candidate Ségolène Royal employed certain references on issues of social order. Finally, the right-wing candidate Nicolas Sarkozy, did not hesitate to rely on the Blair experiment to justify reforms, make fun of an archaic French left, and even adopt some elements of British public policy virtually word for word. How are we to explain these impassioned, divergent interpretations? Tony Blair, who continued to define himself as a progressive and a radical, does not have political friends only on the center-left of politics. Alongside Gerhard Schröder and Bill Clinton, we find José-Maria Aznar, Silvio Berlusconi, George Bush, and Nicolas Sarkozy.

What can a government of the left do today? Leaving aside the countries of northern Europe, in the last decade the governments of Schröder in Germany, Prodi in Italy, and Zapatero in Spain were characterized by the following: important reforms concerning the rights and protection of several categories within the population, such as women, ethnic or sexual minorities, children, and foreigners; an adaptation of social protection that combines restructuring on the one hand and new provisions on the other; greater sensitivity to issues of the environment and sustainable development; reforms in the organization of the state, especially as regards decentralization and European engagement. Moreover, they displayed a certain resistance to the interests and values associated with so-called neoliberalism. They thus proved both favorable and prudent when it came to privatization or the introduction of market mechanisms into ever more extended areas of social life.

By contrast, New Labour proved to be an enthusiastic promoter of enterprise, in the conviction that wealth creation would ultimately benefit everyone. Examination of the Blair governments is an opportunity to reflect on the orientations and projects of the French governmental left and to ponder the impact of public policies over and above speeches and aspirations. We are convinced that politics and government still have a crucial role to play in the leadership, piloting, and transformations of society. This work is neither an indictment, nor an apologia, nor a neutral description. It is a reasoned analysis and critique of the Blair decade.

Consequently, we have chosen to focus on the policies pursued and their impact on society, the economy, and democratic life. In terms of method, we have deliberately skipped over the issue of the origins and ideology of Blairism—a point already well analyzed by numerous works (Crowley, 1999; Finlayson, 2003; Hindmoor, 2004; Mandelson and Liddle, 1998; Blair, 1996). We want to start by observing the Labour governments in action (above and beyond the leader Tony Blair), and the policies they implemented, in order to analyze their outcomes and understand the way in which British society and political life have been transformed.

1 The British Business Model versus the European Social Model

Economic and social policy was the main linchpin of the New Labour project. It justified most of the policies pursued, and a number of assessments focus on this dimension. It was neither a servile adoption of Thatcherite policies, nor a textbook example of good governance according to the criteria of international organizations. Nor was it an updating of British social-democracy, consisting in alleviating the harsh impact of capitalism on individuals, or reducing the most unjust inequalities in terms of wealth and power in the framework of parliamentary democracy. In order to understand the originality of New Labour, we need to remember that the failure of previous Labour governments was primarily economic. Stop-and-go policies had led to erratic fluctuations in interest rates and to inflation's reaching 24 percent in 1975.[1] The Wilson government had to negotiate a loan from the International Monetary Fund, helping to establish a reputation for economic incompetence on the part of Labour.

The New Labour elites were convinced that their credibility and their ability to stay in power were going to be determined by economic issues: they had to reassure both the markets and the middle classes who would swing the results of elections in marginal constituencies. In 1992 Labour lost the elections mainly because of the announcement of tax increases in the budget. Gordon Brown—who was working at the time with John Smith, then in charge of economic affairs for Labour—drew the lesson. In the months that followed, his team published working documents and pamphlets that signaled a major break with the traditional Labour vision.

Impressed by the role of innovation in U.S. growth in the 1990s, he rejected both monetarism and the old Keynesianism. He educated himself in recent economic theory and took a particular interest in new theories of endogenous growth and the logic of globalization. The knowledge economy seemed to open up opportunities for a type of capitalism that was more favorable to individuals, and hence remote from the traditional conflict between capital and labour:[2] the new capital was supposedly composed of individuals' social capital, knowledge, skills, and capacity for initiative.

The discovery of this new mode of capitalist development of knowledge, technological innovation, and globalization inspired radical policies in New Labour. On the other hand, criticism of power structures and power relations was, so to speak, forgotten. The experience of the Blair governments has prompted many debates on the more or less social-democratic or neo-Keynesian character of the reforms accomplished. Relative macroeconomic relative success was qualified by profound imbalances that persisted or deteriorated.[3]

The dynamic of the policies implemented during the decade is key; the "cool Britannia" of May 1997 became "cruel Britannia" in 2005, when Tony Blair decided to become more radical in his reforms. Social-democratic intellectuals like Colin Crouch or David Marquand argued that New Labour had abandoned any reference to the reduction of inequalities or support for the losers from capitalist modernization, and that they identified with the winners, with the new meritocratic, transnational bourgeoisie (Sklair, 2001).

The Activist, Innovative State

In taking their inspiration from new theories of growth, Brown and his team positioned themselves in a framework of neoclassical economic theory, in which markets are competitive, efficient, and dynamic. It was not a question of abolishing the role of the state, but of reorganizing and redirecting its activity so as to benefit from the potential for dynamism and efficiency delivered by markets. Consequently, it was initially necessary to maintain a stable, predictable macroeconomic framework, in order to reassure the markets and appear credible in their eyes. Fiscal, monetary, and budgetary credibility and stability were therefore essential, so as to avoid jolts and negative effects. Next, economic policy must be targeted as closely as possible on individuals, with microeconomic policies of incentives and sanctions (the influence of rational choice theory) to encourage/compel individuals to seize the opportunities offered by the job market and not be dependent on the state.

Gordon Brown's historical success consisted in stabilizing the macroeconomic environment through noninflationary growth, while maintaining a low level of taxation. Compared with other major countries in the European Union, New Labour's economic record was unquestionably exceptional until the crisis in 2008:

- The growth rate of 2.6 percent per annum between 1997 and 2007 was higher than that of the Eurozone, especially France or Germany.
- Inflation averaged 1.5 percent between 1997 and 2006.
- Interest rates were low.
- The unemployment rate fell to around 5 percent, half that of the German or French rates.
- Britain remained the most attractive country in Europe for foreign investors. Every year since the 1990s, it has attracted an uninterrupted flow of investment in firms and services—a key criterion for the dynamic British economy.
- Fiscal and financial policy was prudent, without massive deficits or inopportune tax reductions. The public debt was reduced from 44 to 36 percent of Gross Domestic Product (GDP) (it has since increased to 41 percent), and New Labour committed itself not to exceeding 40 percent of GDP.
- The stock market and property market grew rapidly (a 150 percent increase in property values in nine years), enriching homeowners.
- Thanks to a notable improvement in per capita GDP, Britain rose from last to third place in the G7.[4]

A ten-year period of uninterrupted economic growth, coupled with a stabilization of macroeconomic indicators, is unique in British history. This success was very largely attributable to the chancellor, who was never overruled despite tensions. Nevertheless, Gordon Brown inherited a favorable context from the Conservatives, created after the disaster of Britain's exit from the European Monetary System in 1992. Moreover, at the end of the first Gulf War all European countries enjoyed a bright spell economically. Thus, the phase of economic growth began in 1993 and extended beyond Britain from 1997. The other European countries likewise obtained excellent results during this period in terms of inflation and interest rates; and the Nordic countries grew more rapidly. But even if the gap is not so spectacular vis-à-vis other countries in the Eurozone, Brown was an excellent pilot. Still, these results also have a supranational origin.

The strategy pursued by the chancellor, "Mr. Prudence,"[5] was neither altogether shared nor altogether transparent—two characteristics that frequently irritated the prime minister, Tony Blair. According to Brown, financial markets needed a stable framework, and it was imperative that investors be reassured about medium-term macroeconomic stability. In order to achieve his goals and make New Labour electable, Gordon Brown reversed the usual perceptions and anticipations of economic actors, applying himself to converting his decisions into slogans and dramatizing them:

- In 1996 New Labour committed itself not to increase taxes or public expenditure for two years and to maintain the Conservatives' budgetary framework during the first term.
- Scarcely had he been appointed chancellor of the exchequer than Brown announced that he was committing himself not to manipulate interest rates or let inflation develop in spectacular fashion, by granting independence to the Bank of England. A committee of nine, comprising internal members and others who were external to the bank, would fix interest rates in a transparent way. "Depoliticization" was very popular in the City.[6] The surprise effect was complete.
- He laid down two "golden rules" for British public management: the reduction of debt below 40 percent of GDP and restriction of borrowing to finance public investment (not for current expenditure).

Although he denied being a monetarist like Margaret Thatcher, Chancellor Brown clearly took account of the priorities that his advisors sometimes called a "postmonetarist strategy," combining the struggle against inflation, a strong currency, and iron financial discipline. His economic rigor and his ability to stage his budgets made Gordon Brown a political star particularly appreciated by financial markets and firms. Confronted with a Conservative Party still marked by the disaster of 1992, Brown established an image for himself of recognized economic competence. Year after year he honed his image as a shrewd, rigorous chancellor who inspired respect among the Europeans and in the City. His stature strengthened New Labour's economic credibility and made a decisive contribution to the electoral victories of 2001 and especially 2005, when Blair was in difficulty because of Iraq.

Discreetly, Gordon Brown brought off some neat maneuvers that added substantially to the public coffers without affecting income tax. A windfall tax was voted on companies that manage privatized services such as water or energy. A little later, the national insurance contributions paid by employers were raised to fund the National Health Service (NHS). Numerous tax dodges were abolished in one budget after another. Finally, invitations to tender for the new generation of telephone networks enabled the Treasury to bank around £25 billion. During the first term, the budget was regularly in surplus; not only did this afford an opportunity to reduce debt, but it was an additional argument in favor of New Labour's economic competence.

The price for this financial discipline was paid by the less well off strata. Despite the promise made during the electoral campaign to prioritize education and the regeneration of public services, which had been abandoned by the Conservatives and were in a very poor state, they were left in abeyance. The situation in hospitals and schools deteriorated. In fact, financial rigor was such that public expenditure was not simply frozen at the level projected by the Conservatives for two years, but reduced. Waiting lists lengthened in hospitals, and the NHS was incapable of meeting needs. In addition, as soon as he arrived in government, Brown abolished some benefits for single parents (they were actually very low), which worsened the situation of single mothers with children. Finally, while pensions were among the lowest in Europe, New Labour blocked increases.

The Resumption of Public Investment

The social record of the first term was negligible. Many services, in particular those most in the public eye, such as hospitals and schools, had suffered from underinvestment for years, but the situation deteriorated and redistribution in favor of the poorest was minimal. From 2000 onward, economic success and budgetary surplus made it possible to announce an unprecedented program of public investment. Brown developed a system for piloting public action through information assembled in detailed indicators, allowing him to justify investment by improvements in productivity of the services, management reforms, and recourse to the private sector. The message to the middle and upper classes was clear: public investment is increasing, but the money is being better spent and better managed. To reassure economic actors, Brown demonstrated that he controlled the process and insisted on respect for the economic indicators and forecasts of receipts and expenditure over three years. New Labour's economic competence would not be caught out: Britain would simultaneously experience growth, low inflation and interest rates, and massive investment in health and education. Who can top that? The Conservatives had real difficulty finding chinks in the chancellor's armor.

Total expenditures were announced before the 2001 elections and provided for in the April 2002 budget.[7] In sum, the government planned to invest around £100 billion in public services, particularly health and education. In 2000 health expenditures represented 6.8 percent of GDP, compared with 8 percent in Europe. Blair therefore promised a massive catch-up in the space of a few years: the NHS budget doubled between 1997 and 2005. Following two decades of scarcity, public investment was very considerable. While all-round growth in public expenditure doubled, rising in the next three years to 2.75 percent, the figure was nearly 5 percent for health and education. The share of public expenditure as a percentage of GDP moved upward, rising from 36 percent in 1998 to 44 percent in 2005.[8] By contrast, investment in the social sector, transport, and housing was low. Defense expenditure was not a priority and variations in it were small.

The chancellor's shrewdness did not only consist in this dramatization of a massive investment that was going to enable New Labour to save the public services. Anticipating a change in the economic cycle, Gordon Brown used the investment in countercyclical fashion to maintain growth. In the purest Keynesian tradition, public investment played an important role in job creation: between 1998 and 2003, more than 500,000 jobs were created in the public sector, making it possible to sustain growth. Government borrowing respected the golden rule of public investment and did not finance current expenditure. Obviously, as all specialists on indictors are aware, it is sometimes the case that the difference between the two is essentially a question of presentation. The Treasury teams were not lacking skill in this exercise, even in the reinterpretation of the length of an economic cycle, in order to justify some particular program. The Keynesian minireflation was a success: growth rates were kept at relatively high levels (compared with those of other countries in the Eurozone, particularly France, Germany, and Italy); job creation continued to be sustained; and tax receipts were excellent.

The government likewise committed itself to an ambitious program of building and refurbishment of schools and hospitals, whose objectives are on the way to being realized. The chancellor's shrewdness will have to be assessed in the long term. The use of the PFI (Private Finance Initiative) procedure made it possible to transfer debt and risk to the private sector. Accordingly, this investment does not appear in the sacrosanct macroeconomic balances. Consumers and users (individuals or organizations) will of course pay for using these facilities. But a proportion will be financed by public bodies. As the total debt contracted by the PFI is now rising to more than £7 billion, particularly in health, Gordon Brown's debt indicators are in part an accounting trick (obviously, he is not the only finance minister to have resorted to this kind of practice). We may add that numerous problems persist in the management of these contracts and that, in some cases, the firms involved in such PFI have either earned colossal sums because the contract was highly advantageous to them, or have collapsed leaving sizable unpaid bills. For now, the difficulties involved in public-private partnerships have not been mastered by the public sector. Considerable hidden costs are likely to show up in future years, but the debate cannot be resolved in the foreseeable future.

A Long-Term Project

The effects of these reforms were unquestionably positive: improvement in the health and education services is an *acquis* attributable to the New Labour governments.[9] The first difficulty in drawing a balance sheet derives from the proliferation of performance indicators that render the improvements scarcely credible and difficult to compare. Rather as in George Orwell's *1984*, announcements of progress and performance lose all meaning with the multiplication of indicators.

A few robust assessments clearly indicate a reduction in waiting lists for a whole series of surgical operations and an improvement in emergency reception and within hospitals. Similarly, repeated inspection of schools suggests greater success in exams, a mastery of basic knowledge, and a reduction in class size. However, the record is not as spectacular as was hoped and as measured objectively. It was above all perceptions of improvement that were challenged by the public. The very serious financial crisis of the NHS in 2007, and the program of hospital closures, provoked strikes and discontent on the part of workers and users alike. The closure of schools, university departments, and other services deemed inefficient created opposition and doubts about the reality of improvements. This skepticism induced despair in Tony Blair and his advisers, who did not fail to mobilize a mountain of (more or less relevant) statistics to justify their actions. Thus, during the 2005 election campaign, distrust of leaders and indicators clouded some real successes.

Nevertheless, audits reveal that part of the budget increases went to finance a significant expansion of posts . . . for managers. The complex infrastructure of contracts between different agencies, decentralized budgets, and assessment of performance by inspection regimes, not to mention public-private partnerships—these generated enormous bureaucratic procedures. A very large number of managers were hired to make the new system work. Another part of the budget went to wage increases. Public sector wages had experienced two decades of lean years and heavy constraints, bound up with new agreements in the public sector. In autonomous agencies, or indeed via contracts, a whole range of health and education workers gradually learned the new rules of the game. They became rational, egoistic individuals maximizing their interests, and they succeeded in obtaining substantial wage increases. Doctors—whether general practitioners or specialists—thus enjoyed record salary increases beginning in 2000. Finally, some of the money invested actually subsidized the entry of private firms into public markets at a fairly high cost.

The faith of the New Labour elites in their indicators was naive. By virtue of measuring a whole set of activities on the basis of simplified, aggregate indicators, they ended up believing that such tools, which classify every organization on a scale from 0 to 3, represented reality. In a rational, measurable world, it sufficed to employ the right incentives, the right penalties, and the right rewards—in short, to press the right buttons—to achieve the desired effects. After years of scarcity and underinvestment, it was supposedly enough to invest massively for a few years, with the correct dose of individual constraints and incentives, to obtain results.

This measured social world is a mere fiction: within a few years, New Labour discovered subcontractors of subcontractors that did not provide the service promised by the contract; conflicts arose when the indicators were favorable; individuals learned to cheat the indicators by planning for performance improvements well below those they forecast, so as to surpass their objectives and improve their income; and so on. A massive injection of resources and the proliferation of detailed controls are not enough to make good in three or four years the cumulative arrears in health and education seen in comparison with other European countries.

The New Labour elites did not like the political and social world—its complexity, its tensions, and its conflicts; and they did not always take the trouble to understand social dynamics. They were impatient and wanted rapid change. But revival of the public services is an unfinished project whose results will possibly be apparent only after a decade. New Labour inherited a situation in which the public services were in poor condition, and the first term did not sort things out. What has been an enormous endeavor has in part been spoiled by arrogance and naivety, because complex systems like health or education could not absorb such changes effectively. Multiplying managers, controls, and innovations does not guarantee a quality service at a reasonable cost.

The number of possibilities for measuring human activities by indicators is infinite, but indicators cannot always account for reality—very far from it. New Labour believed in these myths, and radically transformed the role of the state in the social domain. It is no longer the only public service provider. It signs contracts with different organizations to obtain the best performance—the best relationship between cost and service rendered—for citizen-consumers.

Improving Competitiveness

To finance the expenditure of the second term, and despite very hostile media campaigns, Gordon Brown announced tax increases: Value-Added Tax (VAT) and national insurance contributions. Nevertheless, these involved neither income tax nor corporation tax; their rate even fell slightly in 2007. Concerned with the long term, the chancellor was preoccupied with the British economy's lack of competitiveness—a problem to which the Thatcher reforms offered no response. After ten years of Blair government, however, British productivity remained 20 percent lower than that of its European competitors, notwithstanding a set of measures whose effects will perhaps emerge in the long run. It could be that a strategy aimed at including a higher proportion of people in the labor market hurt the productivity figures, whereas the high competitiveness of workers in other countries such as France can also be read negatively, as the ability to put less productive individuals on the dole.

Blair and Brown cast themselves as defenders of enterprise, of a British business model adapted to the pressures of globalization. They encouraged the "Old" Europe to open its eyes and reform its welfare state. Over and above questions of macroeconomic stability and reforms of the labor market, British economic policy consisted of improving the environment for firms, relaxing constraints, resisting demands from Brussels and the trade unions, strengthening competition, and introducing private entrepreneurs and market mechanisms into public activity. This proentrepreneur, proemployer agenda earned Labour a long honeymoon with business circles, significant funding for New Labour, and trade union frustration (Taylor,

2005). Choosing between capital and labor, New Labour was unquestionably on the side of capital. Critical analysis of markets or of the aberrations of firms and employers seems to have been erased. Thus, despite some adjustments in the 1999 law (which preserved the essentials of the laws restricting union activity enacted by Thatcher), and above all following the Warwick accords of 2004 (at a time when the government needed the unions prior to the difficult election of 2005), Britain still has some of the most restrictive trade union legislation in the Organization for Economic Cooperation and Development (OECD).

The Blair governments made themselves the champions of sophisticated regulation of business. Trusting in market mechanisms, they allocated oversight of regulation and control to independent agencies. Brown thus created an agency to regulate financial services (taking over some of the Bank of England's functions), granting it independence, and did the same for the competition authority, the office of fair trading.[10] The government supported changes in the regulation of the privatized services of water, energy, telecoms, and so on. Britain is at the cutting edge of innovation in those domains. It is experimenting with control procedures that enable it to play a major role in the development of European and international norms. Consultancy firms in these areas now export their know-how throughout the world.

Emulating the United States, the government opened its borders to become a country of immigration. Britain is now the symbol of an open labor market, welcoming to young immigrants and especially young Europeans. Around 8 percent of the labor force is foreign today, and London is doubtless the most cosmopolitan capital in the world. On the occasion of the enlargement of the European Union in 2004, Britain was one of three countries to allow hundreds of thousands of Poles to settle. This policy was strongly supported by employers. Most of the 150,000 to 200,000 immigrants who have entered the country each year since 1997 are young and relatively skilled. They easily find work in the London region for low wages. Recently, however, tensions have emerged, and the government has closed its borders to new members of the European Union.[11]

New Labour abandoned the policy of the empty chair adopted by the

Conservatives in protest against adverse European decisions. Its commitment to European integration contrasted with the reserved, even hostile attitude of previous Labour teams. Whereas the Labour Party was a fervent opponent of membership in the Common Market in the 1970s, the policy review launched by Neil Kinnock was at the root of some rethinking. During the 1980s, the development of European social policy proposed by Jacques Delors convinced many members of the Labour Party that the European project was a potential asset to counteract the neoliberal reforms of the Thatcher governments. From the 1990s, the Labour Party used the argument of the Social Charter (limitation of working hours, minimum wage) to convert its activists to the project of European construction. After 1994, New Labour no longer feared that the institutions were inspired by economic liberalism (Hay, 1999). This reorientation of the Labour Party was clear among the MPs who entered the House of Commons after 1983 (Baker and Seawright, 1998). Generally more "Europhile," they saw the role of the United Kingdom in Europe as a sign of "modernity" and an asset for economic development.

Although they presented themselves as pro-European, New Labour's positions need to be qualified. When they were in opposition, Brown and Blair could have compared the merits of the different European social and economic models. The question did not arise. Both were profound admirers of the United States and took an interest in the reforms implemented in Australia and New Zealand. Their view of the European economies was a caricature: they are economies fossilized by the proliferation of rules, which operate with outdated policies. Europe must be a big market, nothing more. In the 1990s Blair and Brown were not interested in the remarkable innovation or success of the Nordic economies, because for them only one model counted—the United States. They were fascinated by that fantastic machine for creating jobs and by the technological innovation and growth derived from the knowledge economy—something that was to become one of the key themes of the Third Way. In other words, to choose between European economies with slower growth, low inequalities, and high unemployment on the one hand, and an American economy with strong growth, high job creation, and high inequalities on the other, the choice was obvious.

Thus the Europeanization of the British economy, observed over the last decade, did not imply adoption of the euro. In response to the challenge of the Conservatives, Blair promised a referendum on the single currency as early as 1996, subjecting it to an assessment of professedly "objective" convergence criteria defined by Brown. For several years, New Labour avoided any commitment or timetable and waited for the prudent chancellor to give his agreement. In 2003 the report of the Begg parliamentary commission allowed him to conclude that the "requisite conditions" had not been met. Gordon Brown was not ready to surrender control of an expanding economy that ensured his reputation.

Incentives and Coercion on the Labor Market

Work was at the heart of New Labour's society and policy. Economic success resulted in falling unemployment and job creation. In a context of macroeconomic stability, employment policy was both innovative and extraordinarily active. It used benefits in order to encourage—and coerce—individuals and households to find a job. These coercive policies were justified by reasons both of economic growth (a higher rate of participation reduces the expenses of the welfare state and increases economic activity) and social integration. In the United States the strategy of incentives-coercion to get people into work is regarded as the most powerful tool in the fight against social exclusion. Various ideological and political reasons pushed Brown and Blair to opt to apply a similar model to the United Kingdom: individuals must seize the opportunities offered to them in the labor market.

Such a strategy is based on two quite distinct elements. The first focuses on developing the supply of market or nonmarket jobs. The rate of employment (that is, the percentage of people with a job among the population of working age) rose from 70.8 percent in 1997 to nearly 75 percent in 2007;[12] unemployment was only 5.5 percent. The improvement in employment conditions was particularly spectacular in the case of young people. Growth certainly made possible the creation of some 2 million jobs between 1997 and 2006 (especially after 2001), but public investment also had a significant impact. In fact, 500,000 posts were created in the public sector. The government constantly banked on supply and removed obstacles that might impede job creation.

The second element of the strategy had as its aim to encourage/compel individuals to accept the jobs offered. Thus the government radically overhauled the organization of public agencies by fusing employment agencies (JobPlus) with the agencies responsible for various benefits (unemployment benefit, single parents, and so forth). The JobPlus agencies benefited from a new dynamic and new means of control. Gordon Brown and his advisers imported the idea of the "Welfare to Work" programs introduced by President Clinton in the United States and, to a lesser degree, Swedish experiments in activating the labor market. The aim was to encourage people to accept a job. The term "incentivization" was the catch word of this policy. To achieve it, the Treasury and the Social Affairs Department progressively revised the rules for granting benefits. This involved encouraging individuals to accept the jobs they were offered with financial incentives (in the form of tax credits or subsidy). Tax credits and certain benefits for children went as a matter of priority to households and individuals with a job; returning to employment did not lead to a loss of those benefits. As someone with a detailed knowledge of capitalism and rational choice theory, Brown understood the importance of coercion to discipline individuals and force them to find work. The novelty of the program derived from its coercive dimension: individuals who refused two or three job offers lost some of their unemployment benefit (and sometimes other benefits as well).

The government took a significant political risk, because this program had no equivalent in Great Britain, and very strong criticisms were voiced from the outset. This Anglo-Saxon version of active employment policy personalized programs to the maximum. But unlike the policies implemented in the Scandinavian countries, the dimension of coercion and sanction was fundamental. At first, criticisms rapidly faded for two reasons: the program was implemented in pragmatic fashion and some of the penalties remained potential; and it achieved its objectives. However, what was involved was a break with the social-democratic idea of universal rights linked to needs or of universal provision, which has also been called into question in the

Nordic countries. In Britain the poor must work; if they behave well, they have a right to the state's active support. If not, they must accept individual responsibility for the fact that they are poor or excluded.

These arrangements initially concerned the long-term unemployed, who are excluded from the labor market and stigmatized by employers. According to Richard Layard, an economist at the London School of Economics and advisor to New Labour, it was also aimed at limiting inflationary pressures in the labor market, because significant numbers of new entries onto the labor market enabled employers to restrict wage increases (cited by Glyn and Wood, 2003). Brown and his advisers streamlined and defined different versions of the program they called the "New Deal,"[13] in order to target the long-term unemployed, single mothers, young people, and so on. Each version of the New Deal combined coercion, penalties, and incentives tailored to the characteristics of each group. Immediately denounced by the left for its illiberal aspects, in practice the program did not create enormous difficulties. In fact, in the early years the New Deal was implemented pragmatically, with little coercion. If the carrot of incentives rapidly worked to the satisfaction of individuals who found a job, and experienced a genuine improvement in their circumstances thanks to tax credits, the stick was handled with a good deal of pragmatism. The coercion associated with this program might have provoked reactions, conflicts, blockages, and made the government unpopular. But its sensitive implementation enabled the government to obtain a positive assessment from the public and beneficiaries of the program.

In a context of job creation and accelerated economic growth, the program speeded up a highly favorable development of the job market. The unemployment rate fell, and this major success by New Labour became the symbol of the Blair governments' effectiveness and pragmatism (solutions that work). These results, however, concealed some rather less brilliant realities. The rate of incarceration of young men from ethnic minorities rose sharply, and Britain held the European record in that regard; according to government estimates, around 4 million people (two or three times the rate of unemployment) were not registered as unemployed and lived off of disability benefits, single parent benefits, and so on. Finally, the New

Deal revealed its limitations in areas where job creation was low. Some of the concentration of high poverty and unemployment was to be found in outlying areas, in formerly industrial towns and cities, the mining valleys of north England, the Midlands, Wales, or Scotland. When the job market is stagnant, a program of incentives and constraints has very little impact, because jobs do not exist. The New Deal was supposed to deal with these issues by creating employment areas enjoying special advantages, particularly at the level of taxation. But the results were negligible. On the other hand, the south and, in particular, the London region benefited from a highly dynamic labor market.

Emboldened by the success of the New Deal, the government then targeted groups that had remained outside the labor market. Such targeting was made with ever increasing precision in pursuit of full employment.[14] From 2002 in particular, the government used penalties and coercion more systematically, ever more aggressively stigmatizing and penalizing individuals who did not get back into the labor market. Ministers sought to compel single mothers of children over the age of twelve, or individuals receiving disability benefits, to take a job by authorizing them to work up to sixteen hours a week without loss of benefits. The technique was always the same: two successive refusals of an offer of work put benefits at risk. In this area, as in others, Tony Blair orchestrated a manifestly illiberal turn in the course of his second term. Rhetoric and programs became more aggressive toward individuals incapable of grasping the opportunities offered them.

Social-Democratic Options?

Margaret Thatcher had accomplished profound reforms of the labor market, by combining massive attacks on the influence of the trade unions with well-nigh total deregulation of the labor market. New Labour soon accepted this legacy and altered it at the margins (Annesley and Gamble, 2004). For Blair especially, particularly opposed as he was to the unions, the antiunion legislation warranted scarcely more than a few adjustments of its most repressive aspects—something that was done in 1999. To the great annoyance of the unions, not only did he not repeal this legislation, but negotiations with economic partners to define the government's economic direction and strategy were conducted in the main with employers. The Department of Trade and Industry created a panel of independent experts to advise the minister on governmental strategy. It included three employers but no trade unionists. This anecdote could be generalized. Brown was less hostile to the unions. He had been a member of the Transport and General Workers Unions (TGWU) in Scotland, and he maintained numerous contacts with trade union leaders. However, when it came to regulating the labor market, the chancellor's views were fairly close to Blair's: the most flexible labor market possible being one of Britain's assets, he systematically opposed union demands.

The principal left-wing measure claimed by New Labour was the minimum wage—an electoral promise that represented its most important concession to the unions. Wishing to depoliticize certain key decisions, the government created a low pay commission to make recommendations to it. Chaired by an academic, its composition was the subject of numerous negotiations in order to limit union influence. Hostile to the measure, employers were represented in force. In the end, the commission proposed a minimum wage in 1999 that was below the level envisaged by the most pessimistic—that is, around £3.60 per hour. The rate was so low that British employers fought the principle of a minimum wage, but adapted to it without great difficulty. At the request of the chancellor, the rate for young people was fixed at a lower level (£3 and then £3.70 in 2001). Despite requests from the commission, Brown resisted increases in these minima exceeding what was a very low rate of inflation up to 2007.[15] Given the slow-down in the creation of jobs, employers secured agreement that increases would not be above inflation.

Despite the government's hesitations, a law on industrial relations was passed in 1999. It marked several advances: the duration of maternity leave was extended, and the protection of women in the labor market improved (albeit without meeting European standards). One of the government's main achievements was clearly the set of arrangements introduced to facilitate family life and working life, in a country where policies for early childhood or in favor of women were virtually nonexistent. A national child-care strategy for small children marked a turning-point. Here Tony Blair proposed various innovative reforms. The presence of a family of four children in the prime minister's residence doubtless helped to advance the image and the reality of a balance between work and family. The generalization of schooling for four-year-olds (and, gradually, three-year-olds), and the rapid development of day care, represented a major innovation in Britain. Around a million places in day care and in nurseries were created between 1997 and 2005. Finally, Gordon Brown made innovations in universal policies, directed at everyone, without any targeting: the state opened an account on the birth of every child, endowed with £250 to which the recipients will have access when they reach their majority; financial benefits were planned for friends or parents who topped up these "baby bonds."

By signing the social chapter of the Maastricht Treaty, New Labour seemed to have accepted the trade union agenda of equal rights for women and worker protection. The creation of structures for consultation with the unions in the case of large firms was briefly considered. On the issue of industrial relations, the Blair governments experienced numerous conflicts with the unions.[16] Certainly, the unions obtained various guarantees regarding their role. Overall, however, New Labour's industrial relations legislation privileged the rights of individuals in firms. Once this initial step had been taken, Tony Blair systematically opposed all attempts to advance various directives guaranteeing minimum rights for workers in a social Europe, whether it be the directive on maximum working hours or the rights of part-time workers. To the astonishment of the employers, the government was even compelled in the latter instance to implement the European directive. With each new directive, the government negotiated at Brussels exemptions involving millions of workers. The Blair governments were unquestionably the most tenacious opponents of attempts at European regulation of the labor market or industrial relations.

In view of the role accorded social capital in a knowledge economy, education policy was a priority to improve the long-term competitiveness of the British economy. Some observers even characterized it as the Labour governments' sole industrial policy. The issue is not insignificant: around one-third of young people still leave school without any training or at the minimum level of the education system. Brown in particular multiplied initiatives to encourage lifelong learning. The government opened up the field beyond schools and universities and created financial incentives (such as the Individual Learning Account) to enable individuals to educate themselves throughout their working lives. Classic New Labour tools were deployed to implement this policy: exclusion of the unions from the negotiations, adoption of the organizational architecture bequeathed by the Conservatives, trust in public-private partnerships and encouragement of them. Most of the programs were aimed at young people in education. Over and above rhetoric and encouragement, this long-term policy is difficult to assess. No notable macro-effect on improvement in education is apparent. But qualitative assessments register an underlying trend toward a renovation of education in the various institutions. Education is no doubt developing in the same way as the numerous education sectors in Britain: a significant improvement in the performance of the better institutions, from which the best qualified benefit; average progress for the rest; and little improvement for the least qualified.

The Issue of Inequalities

While Tony Blair above all prioritized individual opportunities, Gordon Brown regularly referred to the issue of inequalities and improving the condition of the least well off. We must remember that the situation is especially crucial in Great Britain, because Conservative reforms had the effect of increasing inequalities to the point where the country is one of the most unequal in the world.

As a loyal disciple of rational choice approaches, Gordon Brown favored tools that should have precise incentive effects on individuals. Thus, he took a particular interest in tax credits, which also possess the advantage of being pretty much invisible in budgets and thus do not risk scaring middle-class voters. Accordingly, as early as 1998, the chancellor introduced a program of tax credits that reduce child-care costs for working families (especially those on low incomes). This made it possible to work in favor of redistribution toward households with modest incomes, within a more general program favorable to households with children. In one budget after another, Brown increased benefits for children or tax credits for the least well off households. This axis was pursued incrementally but systematically, which had the effect of improving the situation of the least well off 20 percent in Britain—especially those who work. During the first term, the top 10 percent of income-earners (the upper decile), whose income had massively increased over the previous two decades, saw their net income decrease by 1 percent. By contrast, the income of the poorest 10 percent grew by 17 percent. The redistribution was discreet but significant.

During the first term, New Labour, still messianic, frequently announced the emergence of a "new" governance for the "new" millennium. Blair committed himself to abolishing child poverty in thirty years and to lifting a million children out of poverty before the end of the decade. Let us recall that in 1997 Britain virtually held the record for children living below the poverty line—that is, living in households whose income is less than 60 percent of the average. Almost one-third of children at the beginning of the 1990s, the figure still stood at 30 percent in 2000, because Labour's first term did not have much impact in that area. While 3.8 million children were in poverty in 2005–6, their number was reduced to 2.7 million in 2007. In six years, 600,000 children were raised above the poverty line. Despite this improvement, child poverty remained a major scourge, and the performance of the United Kingdom remained poor by comparison with the major Western countries.[17] When a situation is so dramatic, it is not difficult to obtain quantitatively spectacular results with significant levels of investment. The problem consists in pursuing efforts to remedy a structurally problematic situation as regards inequalities. The process initiated by New Labour was not commensurate with the issues. They underestimated the deep springs of poverty in Britain and considerably overestimated the rapidity and impact of the results of their economic policy. Market mechanisms lightly underpinned by the state are not always sufficient to resolve this type of problem. In their defense, however, we should remember that they inherited a catastrophic situation and that getting results in this area is always a medium-term affair.

The program was pursued during the following two terms, but in targeted and limited fashion. As regards incomes, average estimates suggest that the picture has changed during the decade of New Labour government: through the mechanism of redistribution and taxation, the least well off 20 (even 40) percent have seen their annual income increase more rapidly than the 20 percent with the highest incomes.[18] However, the increase in inequality of wealth has not been halted, for several reasons. A highly inegalitarian country, Britain had become relatively egalitarian at the beginning of the 1970s, thanks to a regular reduction in the income of the richest 1 percent (Atkinson and Piketty, 2007). By contrast, at a time when the situation was stabilizing in France in the 1980s, the gaps widened very quickly in Britain on account of developments in the labor market, the property market, and the Conservatives' fiscal policy, which benefited those on high incomes. While New Labour has improved conditions and redistribution in favor of the two bottom deciles, they have left the property market and capital out of account. They have allowed the staggering profits of the financial elites, or the golden handshakes given to the directors of large firms, to drift. Boosted by foreign buyers and City profits, the London property market has exploded in recent years. Property prices, already relatively high, increased more in England than in any other developed country. The quasi-absence of a housing policy (in 2003 Great Britain achieved negative records for house-building—figures not attained since the first part of the twentieth century) only served to compound the pressures on prices. Property has become a major factor in the enrichment of property-owners: the greater the holdings, the higher the gains. The same reasoning applies to the stock market. Enrichment of the richest 10 percent via patrimony was considerable during the New Labour years and canceled out modest fiscal attempts to reduce inequalities.

The calculations of Piketty and Atkinson indicate that the British situation is developing toward an American-style distribution of wealth: the richest 1 percent own 13 percent of wealth, as compared with 17 percent in the United States (2000 figures). However, in sum, taking the period as a whole, while the gaps in capital holdings have increased, the real income of the least well off 40 percent has grown a little more quickly than the income of the 20 or 40 percent richest. Redistribution has occurred, and the contrast with the Thatcher period, with its massive widening of inequalities, is significant. On the other hand, comparison with northern Europe clearly shows that Britain is still one of the most inegalitarian of countries.

The structure of inequalities can be read in all the figures: health indicators, qualifications, position in the labor market. Britain has rapidly flipped over into a system in which poverty is concentrated in pockets that are simultaneously social and spatial. One-third of single women with children do not work. The number of adolescent pregnancies is the highest in Western Europe: around thirty births per thousand young women aged fifteen to nineteen, or three times the European average (the figure is above fifty in the United States). As indicated previously, the rate of poverty among children and old people remains very high. Although the government confronted a serious inheritance on these issues, its mobilization ultimately remained rather limited.

Uneven Achievements

The New Labour governments were responsible for two patent failures: an increase in the north-south divide and an inability to modernize the country's infrastructure, especially in transport.

Ten years of economic growth helped aggravate the imbalances between the north and the south of England. That is not necessarily a problem: growth is a dynamic phenomenon that destabilizes existing systems, and we are not going to lapse into a fetishism of some absolute balance throughout the land. In Britain, economic growth benefits primarily the region of the capital, the extended south-east. By contrast, social problems are concentrated massively in the north, the Midlands, Scotland, and Wales. Most wealth-creation occurs in the south, and, although it denies it, New Labour principally represents the interests of the middle and upper classes. Investment has been directed primarily to modernizing and improving the functioning of the south-east. Thus, in housing, the government declared urban regeneration and house-building programs to be a priority, but at the same time, and more discreetly, it launched massive house-building programs in the London region. The trifling resources of regional development agencies allowed them to do nothing more than administer shortages and organize decline in orderly fashion, without making too many waves.

Despite the regeneration of some towns in the north such as Leeds, Glasgow, Manchester, and now Liverpool, or revitalized capitals like Edinburgh and Cardiff, social problems remain absolutely massive and are concentrated in the north. All the policies for jobs or improving competitiveness came up against this concentration of problems and of urban or regional crisis. The gaps between north and south increased on all economic indicators (even if one finds pockets of prosperity in the north and pockets of poverty in the south).

This unevenness was reinforced by New Labour's timidity when it came to infrastructure. The modernization of the underground or the Eurostar line, and the collapse of Railtrack, are now famous examples of administrative incompetence, but also of a refusal to invest. New Labour opted to maintain competition and private financing: that sometimes yielded positive results, as in the case of airports, but it often increased delays, costs, and a very poor quality of service (as in the case of the railways or the underground). The weaknesses of British transport infrastructure remain spectacular, and road congestion is the worst in Europe. The government chose to multiply tolls to restrict traffic, rather than to invest. It came up against significant mobilizations in protest as a result.

The British economy has become highly speculative, fueled by a property and construction boom (sectors that have generated nearly half the jobs created), financial innovation, and consumption financed by debt. The British certainly profited from phenomenal rises in property prices, but subsequently suffered from them. Thus, from a base of 100 in 1970, the average house price reached around 250 during the property crash of 1990–92; prices then fell below 200 and rose again, to reach 250 in 2000 and 400 in 2005. As a result, household debt to finance the purchase of property grew much more rapidly than incomes. New financial products were developed to allow for indebtedness stretching over forty or fifty years. Massive household borrowing increased in line with house price increase and hyperactive banking lending activities. UK households' debts reached 180 percent of their annual disposable income in 2005 and was still 173 percent in 2009, representing more than 100 percent of the UK GDP.

Extraordinary financial innovation made possible incessant refinancing and a supply of liquid assets to households, because their borrowing capacity was constantly readjusted in line with the potential value of their property. In other words, the consumption boom continued because banks refinanced households by wagering on a continuous rise in property values. But for how long? The dynamism and global success of the City of London attracted investors and were the main motor of New Labour growth. But tensions and imbalances are accumulating, as are the risks. The successor to Gordon Brown at the Treasury will have to be twice as ingenious, all the more so in that the dual constraint of a strong currency and relatively high interest rates once again has handicapped British industry. British industrial output continued to fall during the Labour decade. This deterioration combined with a continuous boom in consumption to yield a trade deficit that has widened year after year. Despite a series of micromeasures favorable to firms and rationalization of research, New Labour definitely did not reinvent an old industrial policy, but nor did it try to revive industry, or the development of new technologies or programs in innovative areas where Britain is well placed, such as biotechnology or the environment.

The program of the Blair governments in the economic and social spheres was composed three-quarters of Anglo-American economic liberalism, with two dashes of social-democracy and a great deal of original experimentation. As Tony Blair left office in June 2007, the balance sheet of the decade looked fairly impressive, but the risks of a crisis were present and structural improvements remained uncertain. The British economy developed unevenly, on the basis of exporting advanced services, the property boom, financial services, and public investment. Productivity remained low, and the trade deficit has never been so large. Inflation went back up over 3.5 percent (more, if property is included); interest rates climbed above the 6 percent mark. Household debt and threats to the property market seem to indicate that a remarkable decade for the British economy is unquestionably coming to a close. A definitive judgment on Labour's management will have to take into account medium- and long-term effects. By way of anecdote, we might add that the Blair governments' late efforts were directed not at high technologies as a priority, but instead . . . at deregulation of the gambling industry, casinos, and on-line betting, which is banned in France and the United States.[19] In June 2007, when Blair left Downing Street, we stated that if the failures regarding competitiveness and development of the economy's industrial base were compounded by a property crash, a rise in inflation, or an unsustainable trade deficit—the Labour record would look decidedly grim.

New Labour was certainly not a classical social-democratic government. It acted massively in favor of capital to promote growth; it disciplined the labor force and was little concerned with inequalities. Redistribution was discreet but significant. Reform of the welfare state was as significant as during the Thatcher period. The social-democratic tradition of universal access to certain benefits was replaced by the rhetoric of individual rights and responsibilities (King, 1999). The change in rhetoric went hand in hand with a change in the policies implemented and a progressively punitive and repressive character to social programs or employment policy. Blair was a convinced disciple of the notion of contract. Social programs and benefits were systematically combined with certain conditions, in a logic of conditionality counterposed to the universality of rights and benefits. It was a case not of "Help yourself and heaven will help you," but "The strong state works to give you opportunities, and your duty is to grasp them. Otherwise, you will be punished." In social policy, but also in health and education policy, that illiberal turn was gradually intensified.

2   Bureaucratic Revolution, or Privatization of Public Services?

For an outsider there is something profoundly puzzling about speeches by the new generation of New Labour ministers and leaders. Among the young forty-year-olds promoted by Tony Blair and Gordon Brown, such as David and Ed Miliband, Ed Balls, Yvette Cooper, and Lord Andrew Adonis, or even Hazel Blears, Beverley Hughes, and Ruth Kelly, we find no flourishes or grand flights of rhetoric, but concrete, specific commitments, costed objectives, a detailed knowledge of their brief, and constant reference to the constraints entailed by the competitiveness of an open, globalized economy. The other side of the coin is that these experienced ministers often express themselves like project heads or organization consultants: everything is codified in terms of performance indicators, aggregate objects formatted in accordance with the canons of the new public management, and a highly rationalist, depoliticized view of public action.

For the Blair and Brown teams, the invention that is "New Labour" served to demonstrate the distance they had put between themselves and previous Labour governments and the unions. As early as 1995, the principal leaders aimed to devise a project for "modernizing" the state that differed from the Conservative project. They promised to regenerate the declining public sector and provide better services, challenge the excesses of competition, and offer protection for employees and workers. They committed themselves to principles of management and responsibility, democratization of public agencies, performance indicators, and a valorization of associations and the "third sector."[1]

Margaret Thatcher's political project had consisted in using the capacities of the state to introduce market or quasi-market mechanisms into public action and impose a new discipline on the British economy: reduction in trade union power, privatization of council housing, cuts in public expenditure. Deregulation and privatization went in tandem with a proliferation and strengthening of rules (reregulation). At the same time, logics of control were reinforced (Hood et al., 1999). For us, this market society must not be defined simply in Marxist terms—as a society in which the ability to resist market mechanisms has been destroyed by restrictive legislation—or, in Gramsci's sense, as a society in which the neoliberal project has become hegemonic. What is involved is a society where the behavior of organizations and individuals in their daily life is orientated, coerced, and aligned with the principles of the market economy (Le Galès and Scott, 2008).

The Thatcher governments centralized and reformed the state, and destroyed traditional social structures (including at the heart of the British establishment, in the organization of the City, or in the legal and medical professions), social solidarities, and institutions. They encouraged actors to behave like egoistic, rational individuals. Establishing rewards and penalties makes it possible to pilot changes in individual and organizational behavior. According to Max Weber, the "bureaucratic revolution" changes individuals "from without" by transforming the conditions to which they must adapt. Bureaucracy is a force for social change, for the destruction of traditional social systems and the creation of new systems, with all that entails in terms of violence and resistance. Bureaucratic rationalization is wholly compatible with modernization of the economy. It makes behavior more predictable and helps create social order organized on the basis of calculation and efficiency.

The bureaucratic revolution initiated by Margaret Thatcher was at the heart of Tony Blair's strategy for modernizing Britain. Her legacy was invoked, taken over, and (of course) modernized. New Labour wanted to put consumers of public services at the center of public services and, to the maximum possible extent, limit the influence of producers—in particular, the public sector unions, which were regarded as one of the most conservative forces in the country. Transformation of the mode of governing—that is, incessant, sometimes contradictory reform of the public sector—was the badge of the Blair governments. It took the form of autonomy for the basic units of public management (schools, hospitals, social services), but flanked by a battery of statistical measures, indicators, and objectives for results or improvements in performance.

Transformation of Public Action and the State Apparatus: The Thatcher Revolution

Whereas Britain was once famous for the stability and adaptability of its political institutions, the Thatcher governments propelled it into "hyper innovation" (Moran, 2003). To reform public administration rapidly, the Thatcher government relied on ideas supported by the economists most opposed to state intervention and on the models of consultants from private management (Saint Martin, 2001). The prime minister herself took it as a given that the world of enterprise should serve as a model for the public sector. The introduction of mechanisms for competition through costs was decisive in the options for transforming the sector. Priority was given to the efficiency and performance of public action. Managers (of services, agencies, and ministerial offices) had individual responsibility for delivery and for obtaining results, that going hand in hand with greater autonomy of budgets and resources (including for managing personnel, who invariably fell outside the restrictions of public sector regulations). Traditional civil service hierarchies were replaced by smaller teams, mobilized for specific projects. Piloting by the center was carried out on the basis of procedures imported from the management of private firms.

With the Conservatives, the instruments of public management in Britain rested on three postulates: the public sector is inefficient; private management is competitive and always superior to public management; introducing competition makes it possible to transfer services to the private sector, which improves managerial efficiency and performance. The definition of criteria, objectives, norms, standards, and performance indicators assumes that everything is objective and measurable—a postulate of hyper-rationalization of a depoliticized world.

In eighteen years of systematic reforms, the Conservatives transformed the country. Their record has no equivalent in Western Europe, where management principles would only be instilled in public action ten years later. The main changes can be synthesized as follows:[2]

- The prime minister became the center of decision-making (Heffernan and Webb, 2005; Heffernan, 2003).
- As early as 1979, the Efficiency Unit and the Scrutiny Program were created alongside the prime minister and the chancellor of the exchequer, in order to require of every public organization the systematic production of performance and efficiency indicators. "Value for money" became the new iron law of British public management, and any program had to be judged in the light of its cost efficiency. Indicators for performance and the introduction of competition had to be produced.
- The classical model of a centralized civil service was transformed by a dynamic of "agencification" (Pollitt et al., 2004), a process of transformation of ministerial offices into autonomous agencies. Some services were hived off. Certain ministries were broken up into autonomous agencies (identified as cost centers and equipped with an accounts department and precise financial objectives).[3] Recruitment and promotion methods were opened up to competition and simplified. Imposing vertical bureaucracies subject to command-and-control instruments gave way to some twelve hundred Quangos (Quasi Nongovernmental Organizations) (Jenkins, 1996). Their heads were appointed by the government or on the basis of criteria laid down by government. Hospitals and schools could "opt out" of the existing system, and the role of locally elected officials in public action was eroded in favor of an unelected elite and consumers. Each agency was responsible for managing its annual budget, and personnel management invariably escaped civil service restrictions; wages varied depending on the agency's performance. In 1997 New Labour inherited a traditional civil service that had

been reduced to around 470,000 (down from 750,000 in 1979), while approximately 350,000 people worked in autonomous agencies.

- Some services were privatized. Internal markets or quasi-markets were created for the production and provision of services within the public sector. Providers and purchasers of services were distinguished, and pursuit of profit became the principle structuring workforce organization and management.

- In 1992 a radical reform of the Private Finance Initiative provided for the financing of public infrastructure (including a hospital or a school) by private capital, in exchange for medium- or long-term revenue, on the model of what already occurred in the case of freeways or bridges.

- Control and regulation of the public sector became more complex. Autonomous agencies were created to produce management indicators according to criteria that were regarded as neutral and independent of local contexts.[4] They were then charged with comparing organizations so as to encourage the spread of "good practice" and penalize bad managers. These reforms presupposed a world in which it is possible to manage social constraints and political conflicts in isolation. The development of techniques for measuring administrative performance provided the impetus for extending practices of inspection and assessment (for example, OFSTED, the Office for Standards in Education, Children's Services and Skills, in the case of education). From an instrument for verifying the use of public money, these bodies turned into the main assessors of public policy and took part in creating incentives and penalties for individuals and organizations. In return, arbitration bodies emerged that encouraged the creation of new rules and codes (Power, 1997). Other organizations were set up to create coherence and guide the behavior of agencies in accordance with the priorities of public policy. In 2000 Britain counted 153 bodies of control-audit-regulation, 50 of them for the local level, or around twenty thousand people and £1 billion a year.[5]

The definition of a set of rules, incentives, penalties, and strict budgetary constraints guided the behavior of actors and autonomous organizations in the direction of efficiency, lower expenditure, and privatization. By following the institutionalized rules, actors became entrepreneurs who act autonomously in the framework of unstable norms (if they were passive, they risked losing their job or their budget). This involved not a retreat by the state, which makes do with being custodian of the rules of the game, but a form of statist centralization that mobilized a new set of instruments (Lascoumes and Le Galès, 2004). This approach was inspired by the utilitarian Bentham, to whom we owe the expression "The more strictly we are watched, the better we behave." Such inspections and indicators also attested to a belief in the superiority of precise, standardized procedures and a lack of trust in individuals who pursue their own interests and respond to the incentives of institutions. The corollaries are distrust of politics, an avowed refusal to take the diversity of social, political, and geographical situations into account, and an instrumentalist and rationalist view of the world.

Think Tanks and the New Labour Elites

The New Labour elite forged its tools for exercising power far removed from the social movements and habitual supporters of the party (for example, feminists or antinuclear activists), or from groups of civil service experts. Their sources of inspiration were in fact to be found on the party's margins, among sympathetic intellectuals who were not always card-carrying members. They constituted a clearly identifiable elite, formed around shared principles and careers. Their main preoccupation was modernization: modernizing the state, politics, and power. "Modernize" and "rationalize" were their catchwords, coined in think tanks. The young MPs elected in 1983 (including Blair and Brown) derived their intellectual and political unity from these think tanks. Since the foundation of the Adam Smith Institute in 1977, these organizations have proliferated, assuming an increasing importance in British political life, especially in the last ten years or so. Originally spaces for independent research and political innovation, they are no longer the preserve of the right. Since 1990, a number of such organizations have emerged on the left—for example, the IPPR (Institute for Public Policy Research, created in 1991) or Demos (1993)—and instill new ideas in the Labour Party.

These think tanks formed a social group in their own right, combining experts, academics, journalists, communications people, and heads from the private sector, but also senior civil servants, who came neither from political groups, social movements, nor trade unions. They shared a distrust of trade unions, of local authorities and their paternalistic, redistributive mode of government, and of regionalisms and social movements. They conceived of themselves as a governmental left. While Thatcher was giving autonomy to the central state and reducing local powers, they were preparing a riposte. They were aided in this by frequent exchanges with circles close to Bill Clinton, which were themselves orientated toward Europe— that is, primarily, England. Within this universe, networks were formed that participated not only in reflection but also, progressively, in action. Think tanks served as a recruiting ground for New Labour ministers or advisors— for example, Geoff Mulgan, Mathew Taylor, and David Miliband.[6] Out of the public eye, they prepared reports and policy proposals that informed and often inspired government policy. Demos and the IPPR, in particular, genuinely contributed to political thinking; they partially replaced the work of politicians (parties and MPs), civil servants, and academics.

Since the end of the 1970s, relations between government and the world of business have been transformed under the impetus, in particular, of the privatization and deregulation campaigns started by Thatcher. After nearly twenty years of growth, the financing of these think tanks, which enjoy the status of charitable body, is beginning to raise questions. Financed mainly by foundations, some of their funds currently derive from big multinationals. This development forms part of the logic of interpenetration between the public and the private and the naturalization of the business model.

With the state becoming predominantly a market regulator, lobbying has become one of the best means of influencing political decisions and hence preserving a competitive advantage (Harris, 2002). New forms of democratic management have been introduced, involving a partnership with firms and associations in new policy development networks. Over and above think tanks, the New Labour elites took over agencies, public relations, and consultancy. Several lobbying firms (for example, Lawson Lucas Mendelsohn—LLM—Good Relations, and Portland PR) were founded by people close to the Labour Party. A number of former political advisors circulated between lobbying firms, the party, and the government: Colin Byrne (former number two to Peter Mandelson in the Communications Unit); Jo Moore (former party press officer, subsequently in the Transport Department); David Hill (Labour Party head of communications between 1991 and 1999; this close collaborator of Tony Blair became a director of Good Relations Ltd.,[7] before succeeding Alastair Campbell in 2003 as the prime minister's head of communications). For election campaigns, Labour (and the Conservatives) enjoyed the free services of important lobbyists, "on leave" from their firm, which they later rejoined. The two parties thus benefited from highly qualified personnel who were involved in power networks. The clients of lobbying firms were able to secure direct access to the heart of government.

These networks and teams defined the new representations and practices of public action and public services for New Labour, in a very different way from the habitual modes of senior civil servants or trade unions.

"Activist" Governments

The New Labour team elected in 1997 was largely won over to the rather vague theses of "new public management." These resulted in the application of the principles of rational choice and classical microeconomics to public management, sometimes by transferring the recipes of private management to public management. Blair and Brown clearly understood that a redefinition of the rules of political action (in the direction of the regulatory state) went hand in hand with an increase in controls. While part of the traditional bureaucracy was dismantled and subjected to market mechanisms, the core executive gained in independence.[8] The new government did not intend to reconsider the framework of public management left by the Conservatives. The inheritance was adopted, mobilized, and consolidated by the Blair governments, whose action can be characterized as follows:

- Indicators for good public management extending beyond performance were developed for the precise piloting of public action.
- According to the social model of neoclassical economists, individuals respond to stimulation.
- The delivery of public policy combined public and private partners in flexible ways.
- Priority was given to delivery and the definition of objectives.
- Power was centralized in order to initiate reforms, monitor delivery, and make government action coherent.
- The inspiration for reforms no longer derived from the senior civil service, but from think tanks, experts, consultants, academics, and foreign experience (essentially the United States).

When they took office in 1997, neither Tony Blair nor Gordon Brown had any experience of government. But they had honed their weapons as reformers in the Labour Party. During the first term, they developed mechanisms for controlling, joining up, and coordinating government action, which was decidedly fragmented after two decades of privatization, the creation of agencies, and the introduction of competition mechanisms. Their action was in line with that of the Conservative governments, as indicated in the white paper *Modernising Government*, published by the government in 1999. At the outset public investment was regarded with suspicion, and the analytical framework of management (in its new public management version) was widely assimilated and advocated. On the other hand, blind confidence in the superiority of the market economy, at all times and in every instance, was rejected; privatization and competition, particularly in the area of health, were initially limited.

The new criteria for good management were called "Best Value for Money," inspired by thinking on public management developed by U.S. Democrats and within the Clinton team. The New Labour elites wanted to introduce a center-left vision of good management, by expanding the range of objectives, especially in social terms, of quality of service provided, even of sustainable development. They tried to identify management tools that make it possible to compel public organizations to improve their management and service provision, but also to allow them greater freedom to define their priorities and achieve their objectives. Performance and efficiency took on a less economic meaning. Modernization of the public sector aimed at improving performance through the use of a centralizing instrument to compel, measure, and penalize.

Because a government is always crisscrossed by contradictory logics, the delivery of public action reveals the multiplicity of actors, interests, representations, and interpretations; New Labour wanted to put an end to the dilution of political responsibility and bureaucratic fragmentation (Massey and Piper, 2005). They foregrounded notions of "joined-up government" (government through the sharing of the resources of different departmental sections) (Bogdanor, 2005), and then partnership, which refer to the idea of coordination between different organizations. Collective public action had to be visible to the citizen.

Finally, New Labour called into question the clientelist system for appointing agency heads and members of the board of directors of different organizations. In contrast to the last years of the Major government, marked by corruption scandals or unjustified party appointments, Blair cast himself as the champion of honesty. Appointment procedures were made more transparent, and New Labour encouraged the promotion of women and representatives of ethnic minorities to leadership positions. The renewal of leaders in the public and quasi-public sector was profound and created a dynamic for delivery of the New Labour program. The diversity in the backgrounds of the new leaders, who came from local authorities, the voluntary sector, or sometimes the private sector, even of trade unions, represented a break with traditional British leaders.

The dynamic of joined-up government justified the creation of new specialist organizations to make public action visible: the Low Pay Unit, for example, or the Women's Unit (an organization responsible for promoting women). The new programs had eloquent names that sounded like slogans: Crime Reduction Programme or Anti-Drug Programme. Some two hundred specialist task forces were in existence by the end of Blair's first term (Richards and Smith, 2004).

To revive investment in the public services after 2001, New Labour generalized public-private partnerships via the PFI (Private Finance Initiative), which had been invented by the Conservatives to encourage the role of the private sector in public services and reduce public debt. Part of the investment is taken on by the state and the other by private investors, who build the facilities and manage them for a period of twenty to thirty years (one of the objectives is a better long-term use of resources). Their remuneration during the whole period is fixed by contract. Given that the facilities remain public, we cannot follow the trade unions and speak of covert privatization. On the other hand, the managerial methods used in these enterprises are not the same as those in the public sector, and the employees belong to the private sector. Although the initial balance sheet of school and prison building on this model was mixed, the Treasury encouraged recourse to PFI in order to make new public facilities possible. In 2000 the government committed itself to building (or renovating) five hundred schools and one hundred hospitals before 2010, limiting the impact of this revival of investment on the public accounts (and the debt ratio), and this despite profound opposition from within the party, particularly from the public sector unions, which vigorously denounced the logic of "build now, pay later." In 2005, sixty-eight hospitals were finished, sixty-four of them financed by the PFI. The completion of buildings in a fairly short period of time is also evidence of efficiency: such a program would have been difficult to accomplish in the public sector.

Debate on the efficiency of the PFI is particularly heated. Critics have stressed that proof of better use of resources in the framework of a PFI has not been forthcoming. Fairly widespread cases of spectacular loss of financial control, questionable management, inefficient subcontractors, or firms getting rich because of badly drafted contracts, have demonstrated the difficulty of controlling the public sector when it transfers the risk to the private sector. The costs of managing these contracts, and of paying for provisos that were not anticipated at the outset, are also very high. The National Audit Office has emphasized the cost reductions, but also the medium-term risks and uncertainties. However, all this does not guarantee a better service, though it can contribute to it. It is too soon to construct a detailed balance sheet.

The PFI introduced the private sector into the management of health services. The agreement signed in 2000 with an association of private firms by the ultra-Blairite Alan Milburn made a gradual reduction in waiting lists possible. Significant groups for private management of health services involved in the PFI were constituted. Capita, Accord, or Serco, for example, responded to outsourcing projects, because profit rates were very high for anyone capable of managing financial plans and complex operations. In 2005 the private sector was responsible for 4 percent of NHS treatments, and the government fixed a target of 15 percent by 2008. Diversification in service providers was supposed to increase individual choice and create competition between different organizations (Driver, 2006). But in the final analysis, uncertainty persists: was the government in the process of privatizing the public health sector? Or, on the contrary, was it on the way to nationalizing the whole sector and including the private sector in central government's targets via contracts for objectives? In fact, the old system was based on a dichotomy between the completely public and the completely private (which grew over the years). New Labour hoped to control the whole system through objectives determined by government and thus, thanks to piloting by the center, to encompass the private system as an object of public action. Strengthened in a direction and on the basis of objectives determined by the government, competition would facilitate an improvement in the quality of health provision—something that has indeed occurred.

Do these developments improve the services provided to the patient or create new inequalities? The fragmentation of provision, and the secrecy associated with the contractual transactions, render a systematic evaluation of these initiatives particularly difficult and, as of now, inconclusive. There is a risk of an American-style drift (very high costs to care properly for a small proportion of the population). But a bad outcome is not inevitable. It is not impossible that once the learning process has been completed, the NHS will succeed in significantly improving the provision and quality of health services. The British system of health care, formerly a cause for pride, profoundly deteriorated during years of underinvestment by the Conservatives, to become one of the worst in Western Europe. New

Labour made significant investment and wagered on choice for consumers and piloting by indicators, by introducing market mechanisms and private actors.

Control through Information

"Welcome to target world," the enchanted world of performance indicators (Hood, 2006). New Labour systematized a way of steering government on the basis of performance objectives, league tables, and strict financial control. These developments revealed their credence in the magical powers of synthetic indicators to bring about rapid changes. Moreover, this was one of the characteristics of New Labour management: radical reforms were conducted through a proliferation of indicators and a rapid redefinition of targets and programs. In their eyes, the social world was malleable, reactive, and dynamic. Under pressure, it reacts forthwith to commands for mobilization from the masters of the moment. One cannot but be surprised by the extraordinary ambition of piloting society through such indicators, and the discrepancy as regards service provision to the population.[9]

Thus, as early as 1998 the government announced the creation of three hundred performance objectives for all departments. Each of them might make for newspaper headlines. These objectives were bound up with the resources allocated by the Treasury; each was then divided up into dozens or hundreds of specific indicators by area.

In view of the importance of the rhetoric of modernization, New Labour made it a point of pride to mobilize every "modern" technique, not just the latest managerial fashions but also the systematic production of aggregate indicators thanks to increasingly sophisticated new technologies. They promoted with enthusiasm the development of e-government. Following the example of the managerial software used in large firms to know the activity of different units in real time, they generalized the activity of reporting from agency or unit heads to the lowest level.[10] While this made the fortune of large consultancy firms that promised miracles thanks to the use of new systems of information management, the enthusiasm of the Labour elites experienced some sensational fiascos, like that of the NHS's centralized information system. We should nevertheless recall that the British do not have a monopoly on disasters in this area.

New Labour wanted to increase the coherence of government action, formerly dependent on large departments that were solely responsible for delivery of their policies. A new group—the Delivery Unit—was created in 2001 (in the office of the prime minister and in close contact with the Treasury) in order to put the heads of the different departments under pressure. Each service had to commit itself to a plan (Public Services Agreement) fixing objectives and performance indicators. This procedure made it possible for the prime minister's teams to monitor the delivery of different policies closely, particularly in sensitive sectors such as heath, education, policing, transport, and the environment. The prime minister and the chancellor thus discovered a capacity for spurring and precise monitoring. Some political commitments were met in the time promised—for example, the creation of school places for all four-year-olds. In the area of health the government wanted to revise hospital management indicators in 2000, so as to mark the difference from Conservative management. The strategic document on the plan for the NHS, "a programme of investment, a programme of reforms," detailed the set of management objectives, taking account of indicators such as waiting times in accident and emergency wards, or the delay in getting an appointment with a specialist or an operation. Precise, detailed objectives were set out for the directors of hospitals, services, doctors, and nurses. The government created a National Institute for Clinical Excellence (NICE) to measure the costs and effects of treatments, and a specialist control body—the Commission for Health Improvement— to measure performance and assess hospitals. Health care provision was streamlined.

Furthermore, in each area the government wanted to reward good pupils and penalize the others. This aspect of rationalization was central in New Labour's conception of public management. League tables were a classical instrument of the "new public management." Already used for schools, the system was extended to hospitals. Thus, a league table of hospitals was published for the first time in 2001 by the health secretary, and then reassessed every two years. Competition, the rush to measured performance, and a system of penalties and rewards often had the effect of mobilizing actors in the direction desired by the system's promoters. The objective of absolute rationalization led to a uniform system of grading (ranging from 0 to 3) with a set of parameters that lacked any coherence. All hospitals (170 on the first occasion) were thus ranked in four categories—no stars, one star, two stars, and three stars—on the basis of the following criteria, all of which were translated into performance indicators.

Hospitals were graded 0–3 on twenty criteria, including:

- waiting time for emergencies and appointments;
- number of patients who, when their operation has been canceled, have still not been operated on twenty-eight days later;
- cleanliness;
- the number of patients who wait longer than two weeks for an appointment with a cancer specialist when their GP has detected a risk and cites the urgency of an examination;
- the number of deaths (per 100,000 operations), calculated as a percentage, in the thirty days subsequent to a heart operation;
- the number of emergency readmissions for those discharged from hospital;
- the elimination of infections caught in hospital;
- the abolition of mixed wards;
- patient satisfaction;
- the percentage of patients whose transfer to a different hospital for medical reasons has been delayed;
- the percentage of absent staff.

In 2001, thirty-five hospitals obtained three stars, while twelve received no stars. The latter were immediately placed under the direct control of the new NHS Modernisation Agency, charged with reorganizing a hospital to improve its management and efficiency. Penalties in individual cases were thus very real. The media especially stigmatized the St. Helier NHS Trust, identified at the time as the worst hospital in Britain, and deprecated the poor ranking of the highly prestigious Oxford Radcliffe Hospital Trust. Conversely, the hospitals with the best results became the benchmark against which to compare the management of the rest. The following year, the directors of "three star" hospitals secured considerable managerial autonomy, greater financial resources, and the freedom to develop their activities. Directors of "two star" hospitals likewise received somewhat greater resources, but no additional managerial autonomy. The secretary of state officially encouraged the departure of directors responsible for poor services, if they did not significantly improve their performance the following year. Finally, some services, and then some hospitals, were closed.

The system of penalties was put in place very gradually. Hospital closures were inconceivable during the Thatcher governments. But the routinization of league tables legitimated penalties—that is, closure of a hospital. However, that continued to be systematically challenged at a local level and was supposed to be applied only in order to ensure patient safety and guarantee an improvement in the major centers on which resources were focused. However, the effect of such measures remains to be assessed. Fifteen hospitals have been closed since 1997. After a phase of investment, budgetary rigor threatened sixty hospitals in deficit with closure, when it was envisaged concentrating resources and advanced technologies in a few enormous flagship hospitals.

The same approach prevailed in numerous areas of public action: primary and secondary education, higher education, the environment, social services, and so on. The logic of the audit and inspection progressively led to more standardization, with the "managerial" dimension getting the upper hand over the more political dimension of administration; the pressure on workforces was increasingly strong. Strategic priorities, the needs of local populations, and political choices were set aside, in favor of competition to obtain the maximum score, which counted as political and professional success.

During the first term, the government was above all taken up with the issue of education. But financial prudence prevailed, and investment remained limited. From 2001 onward, improving public services became the priority. The Conservative Party and the media increasingly attacked the government, which was thought to be obsessed with control and supervision. The multiplication of targets and strategic objectives in all areas became a caricature, especially when a senior minister explained that the government's objective was to reduce the number of objectives in public management!

Several reports were drawn up inside and outside government: the accumulation of audits had had unintended negative consequences; the sectoral approach to control had led to an excessive centralization of norms and standards, as well as a fragmentation of local public management, without any notable improvement in local public services. Tony Blair and Gordon Brown then undertook a program of public investment, accompanied by tax increases and redistribution to the poorest households. However, to get this program past the middle classes of southern England in particular, the government was obliged to provide, as rapidly as possible, measurements of the efficiency of this expenditure, which was sharply criticized by the opposition. New tools of management were therefore invented in different sectors. Thus, local government was supposed to respond to criticisms of the bureaucratic nightmare of data production and the control of strict procedures of "good management." Hyper-rationalization and simplification were the principles that underlay the production of simplified synthetic indicators, making it possible after 2001 to establish public management analysis charts, in order to convince the public of the soundness and efficiency of the public investment that had been made. The idea was that the quality of public services is an issue for the public: citizen-consumers must compare service providers and penalize elected officials or inefficient organizations. The pressure for change was thus twofold: it derived from both government and consumers.

Adopting an idea developed by the Conservatives, from 2004 onward New Labour encouraged the "best" hospitals to opt out of the public system and become foundations enjoying greater managerial autonomy—especially to borrow capital—while entering into contracts with the NHS. Furthermore, private groups were authorized and encouraged to take over some hospital activities so as to improve performance indicators. Tony Blair suggested that all English hospitals could become autonomous by 2008, but this prospect sparked heated debates in the House of Commons and the Labour Party. Public-private partnerships were also adopted to improve problem schools in socially difficult areas (Education Action Zones), to prompt innovation, to diversify educational provision, and to expand parental "choice." These City Academies were in part financed by private funds, but access to them was free. They had autonomy in terms of management and pedagogy (even if they had to follow the national curriculum), or for a part of their curriculum. Whether religious or not, they were managed by boards of directors and selected their pupils.[11] However, the results were very mixed, and some of the plans were abandoned. University reform also created internal frictions among the majority. University enrollment fees were sharply increased and will rise still further if the most prestigious universities, which want to compete with the major American universities, have their way.[12] The reform of university funding was based on establishing loans for students and sophisticated repayment mechanisms.

Auditing Society

Assessment of public policy is essential in a democracy and a major trend of transformation. New Labour's particularity consisted in generalizing such assessments, above all in the tightest form of control—the audit.

Thus, the culture of the audit, which derived from firms, was gradually transferred to all areas of British public life and affected political parties, associations, and charitable organizations alike. While the government decentralized public service provision, and encouraged the participation of the voluntary sector in managing public services, it combined this decentralization with new quid pro quos. All sectors were henceforth subject to an assessment of their performance and procedures. The illusion of the total "inspectability" of society betrayed the influence of the utilitarianism of the philosopher Jeremy Bentham. But the proliferation of audits eroded trust in the professional ethic and the sense of public service. Social control of this kind contradicts the idea that everyone acts in good faith and destroys trust in the competence of social actors.

When it came to organizations, one consequence of the streamlining of procedures was deterioration in the morale of employees and a decline in ethics (Meyer and Rowan, 1977: 359). Are teachers those best qualified to assess students? Are doctors best placed to judge the treatment to be given to their patients and priorities in allocating medical resources? Transparency was regarded as the requisite accompaniment of any contribution. How can the generous donor be certain that the money given to charitable organizations will be spent in optimal fashion? New organizations emerged to audit the many bodies in receipt of money from the public or from public funds. The implications are the same in politics. If the leaders of political parties cannot trust their activists, why should the public trust them? The dream of some absolute bookkeeping (standardizing, measuring, assessing, comparing, penalizing) is opposed to the trust that is indispensable to the operation of representative institutions. The publication of audits is supposed to increase transparency and hence users' ability to choose. But it can also reveal problems when there are no guarantees that effective measures will be taken. In this sense, transparency can encourage apathy rather than action.

The audit has become natural in British society. Control is now present at all levels of social and political life.[13] It transfers the management of uncertainty, especially economic uncertainty, from political authorities to individuals. The constant invocation of individual responsibility, which is the quid pro quo of the logic of multiplying the choices offered to the citizen-consumer, aids the internalization of controls and the adoption of individualistic strategies that rupture existing solidarities or loyalties. Summoned to take responsibility for the costs of their choices, individuals cannot be the counterpowers formerly represented by groups. When the audit does not yield satisfactory results, it is rarely the audit itself that is called into question, but instead the skills of the auditors. The whole of society is affected: political parties, agencies, schools, associations, and even the Church of England.[14] The routinization of auditing also affected research: works like "The Audit of Political Power and Democratic Control"[15] or "The Audit of Citizenship"[16] obtained public funding.

New Labour public management drew on the Conservative legacy to develop an original model of public service reform, on the basis of altering service providers and introducing logics of choice and competition. A succession of reforms accompanied a revival in public investment. The Blair government was not favorable to universal, free public services. Many innovations were made, combining in experimental forms elements of the public sector with elements of the private sector for service provision, the totality within a framework controlled by the government. No country in the world has thus far propelled such a radical experiment in piloting by performance indicators and targets—something that arouses a lot of interest on the part of the OECD or the World Bank and allows British consultants to export their know-how throughout the world. The quality of services has improved in health and education, but part of the population has been progressively marginalized. Some services in difficulty offer benefits only of a very low quality. The original combination of control by indicators and autonomy to enhance dynamism played a role in innovations in management and an improvement in some services. In other instances such control was an illusion, and piloting by indicators and incessant changes created an image of change in the case of services that were in fact deteriorating. While the experiment was interesting, New Labour's greatest error was unquestionably that it gave undue credence to the myth of rationalizing and inspecting society. Research underway reveals, on the one hand, errors of measurement and, on the other, the large variety of strategies developed by actors to distort the results.[17] No doubt some fine minds are soon going to propose a new generation of indicators to correct the failings of the previous indicators, but the conservatives have also been struck by the limits of "government by numbers" and, if elected in 2010, will probably in part challenge the system.

The British example invites us to go beyond the traditional opposition between market regulation and political regulation: market relations do not necessarily disrupt hierarchical relations or power relations. In fact, the state can play a central role in introducing market mechanisms and consolidating social inequalities and power relations.

3 Decentralizing or Centralizing Institutions?

Analysis of the New Labour "hybrid" sometimes runs into intractable contradictions. Thus, the British press violently attacked the alleged centralizers Tony Blair and Gordon Brown for contravening the principles of the unwritten Constitution and the balance of powers. By contrast, reforms of parliamentary procedure and the creation of parliaments and executive governments in Edinburgh and Cardiff were clear evidence of progress toward a more decentralized and democratic form of government. This tension is especially illuminating for an understanding of the dynamic of Tony Blair's governments.

As soon as it was elected, the Blair government announced what seemed at the time to be an institutional revolution: the election of assemblies for Scotland, Wales, and Northern Ireland; a drastic reform of the House of Lords; a law on freedom of information; the signature of the European Convention on Human Rights; the creation of regional development agencies and the restoration of an elected metropolitan government for London. "Modernization" of the Constitution thus represented a major program, marking a turning point for the United Kingdom. Blair appeared to be a major reformer on a terrain neglected by the Conservatives, modernizing a hypercentralized regime, some of whose elements seemed archaic. These changes took place against a background influenced by the will to seize the opportunities provided by membership in the European Union. Thus Blair also promoted a new positive and proactive attitude toward European partners, in contrast with his Conservative predecessors. The strategy of "placing Britain back at the heart of Europe" involved concessions to the process of European integration and the adaptation of Whitehall, eroding the sovereignty of the British Parliament from the top and contributing to increase the role of the executive as the conduit of the Europeanization process.

A decade later, and the outcome is strangely controversial. Having signed the law on freedom of information and the European Convention on Human Rights, in the last years of his term Blair pushed through a set of laws that ran counter to his professed liberalism. Despite the creation of parliaments at Edinburgh and Cardiff, Blair seemed more than ever the prime minister of southern England, ill at ease with his creations and indifferent to the widening gaps between the London region and the rest of the country. Having created a metropolitan government in London, he clumsily sought to control the electoral process for selecting the candidate and found himself with an old enemy, Ken Livingstone, in London's town hall. The creation of regional development agencies, although announced as a major advance in decentralizing government, is now held up as a semifailure, given the process of centralization of government activity. Following minireforms in incomplete stages, the reform of the House of Lords is still to be completed. The introduction of a dose of proportional representation for some elections (for example, the Scottish Parliament) seemed to herald an unlocking of the political system, but all innovations in that direction were later abandoned. The "most European of British prime ministers" left Downing Street without having secured the adoption of the euro, or made substantial progress in fostering a positive debate about the position of Britain in the EU. The referendum promised in 2004 on the EU Constitution lost its raison d'être after the French and Dutch electorates voted against it in 2005, to the greatest relief of Tony Blair. His last European summit, in June 2007, saw him in an isolated position, "chastised by the Germans for resisting an EU charter of human rights, lambasted by the Austrians for opposing guarantees on welfare, criticized by the Bulgarians for going back on a constitutional treaty he'd signed up to three years ago."[1]

New Labour initiated an ambitious reform program, but in retrospect what is striking is the lack of preparation of institutional reforms, their ad hoc justification, the short-term tinkering, and the contradictions between different models, elements of which involved genuine innovations that were never fully delivered (Flinders, 2006). The new laws on information, human rights, and justice were always accompanied by a series of exemptions that permitted nonapplication of the text, justifications for preserving government privileges. The direction of change and its delivery indicate that the Blair governments were eager to appear more open, but in reality defended their interests, manipulated the terms of reference, and proved incapable of providing an overall vision. Territorial questions, which are essential in Britain, were dealt with in accordance with the interests of the moment, without an overall perspective on the political community of the United Kingdom. By contrast, processes of centralization of the powers of control and leadership were systematically and rationally strengthened at the level of prime minister and chancellor of the exchequer, to make possible the mobilization of the activist state, even if the rivalry between the two men limited the risks of abuse of power. This contrast makes it possible to see the New Labour project in a new light, by bringing out the strength of the activist state and the weakness of the political conception of the union, which went hand in hand with a deep distrust of local and regional government.

Polycentric and Asymmetrical Governance

Once a country of stable, bureaucratized, and nonpoliticized local government, the United Kingdom became, during the Thatcher period, the most centralized country in Europe. Numerous experiments had destabilized and undermined local institutions (Stoker, 2004), and expectations of the new Labour Party were therefore very high. New Labour was committed to setting in motion a process called devolution, which made it possible to preserve a unitary state in law while more or less extensive powers were entrusted by central government to regional authorities—or national authorities, if one believes, as is the case in rugby and football, that Scotland, Wales, and Ireland are separate nations. This transfer of power was not enshrined in the Constitution and can therefore be reversed. The 1998 devolution, an asymmetrical and complicated system (each territory is governed by different rules), was clearly distinguished from both Belgian- or German-style federalism and decentralization in the French manner.

The former Labour leader, John Smith, had committed Labour to promote devolution. Tony Blair honored the promise without hesitation but also without tact. He attempted to impose his choices or his men on Welsh and Scottish Labour organizations or in London. Such interference earned him some bitter political setbacks, and he was thus the paradoxical hero of a process with which he was never very at ease. He introduced very significant reforms without having any special interest in the issue, even with a certain reluctance. In fact, New Labour had to pay its debt to the Scottish and the Welsh, who had kept the party afloat during the dark years and inflicted resounding political defeats on the Conservatives. (For the record, let us remember that in 1997 the Conservatives no longer had a single MP in Scotland.)

Devolution in Scotland and Wales

In line with their electoral promises, New Labour organized prelegislative referendums in Scotland and Wales in the months that followed their victory. There was a clear-cut majority in the first case, a narrow one in the second,[2] and the powers devolved would reflect this unequal enthusiasm. New Labour then rapidly and effectively accomplished a process of devolution, by passing laws in 1998 that created a parliament in Edinburgh and an assembly in Cardiff, and by organizing the first elections in 1999 with a new electoral system, the additional member system.[3] The results marginalized the Conservatives that little bit more and were generally favorable to Labour, although the votes did not produce outright majorities.

The "devolved" governments are more or less autonomous and led in Scotland and Wales by a first minister (not to be confused with the British prime minister). The great man of Scottish Labour, Donald Dewar, took the head of the executive in Scotland; on his death in 2000, he was replaced by Henry McLeish and then by Jack McDonnell. In Wales, Blair imposed one of his collaborators, Alun Michael; soon defeated by a vote of no confidence of the Welsh assembly, he was replaced by the historical leader Rhodri Morgan.

Scotland, a "nation without a state" in the words of Jacques Leruez (1983), had preserved a culture and institutions that differ from those of England (particularly the Church, part of the legal system, and the education system). Over several decades a desire for autonomy, even independence, had developed. After the upsurge of the 1970s, Jim Callaghan's Labour government (in a pact with the Liberals) had failed in a first attempt at devolution, with the 1979 referendum. In the 1980s the independence party (the Scottish National Party) was reinvigorated, galvanized by visceral opposition to the government of Margaret Thatcher. The Scottish Labour Party (like the trade union movement) also gradually came to plead for a form of decentralization and the creation of a Scottish parliament and government. Various opinion polls regularly registered a desire for greater autonomy, and sometimes independence, within the European Union. A smaller movement also developed in Wales, around the nationalist party Plaid Cymru.

The status provided for Scotland allocated it a budget of £20 billion or more, and legislative powers over health, education, transport, housing, law, agriculture, and the environment. By contrast, issues of foreign policy, defense, social security, immigration, and economic policy were strictly reserved for the central government in London and the Westminster Parliament. The main constraint is power over taxation, which can vary only marginally vis-à-vis the rate fixed for Britain—something that strictly limits the possibility of increasing public expenditure.

The status and budget provided for Wales are significantly more restricted, just like political sentiment in favor of devolution.

The administration of the Scottish Office at Edinburgh came under the control of the Scottish first minister elected by the Parliament. In London, the Department of Constitutional Affairs is now responsible for the affairs of the Celtic peripheries.

The dynamic of devolution led to forms of government and political priorities that were rather different from New Labour's (Jeffrey and Wincott, 2006; Greer, 2006). The introduction of a dose of proportional representation facilitated the emergence of new parties (the Greens), who entered the assemblies or obtained representation that allowed them to disrupt the traditional balance of power. Moreover, nationalists became the main opposition parties in both Wales and Scotland. These developments underlined the distortions in the British national electoral system, which allows the victorious party to rule single-handedly with the support of one-third of the electorate. As a result, the legitimacy of Westminster dualism (and "elective dictatorship") was eroded (Bennie and Clark, 2003). The early stages of the Scottish Parliament were marked by a desire to escape the systematic opposition between two dominant parties, into a system more open than that of Westminster. Thus the parties cooperated even before the elections, and the first government was a coalition between Labour and Liberal Democrats, which raised scarcely any qualms (Paterson et al., 2001). By contrast, Welsh politics remained dominated by the Labour Party in its traditional form, highly regionalized and nonpluralistic. Two years had to pass before Labour opened the minority executive up to the Liberal Democrats, who were the fourth largest party in the Assembly.

The effects were clear as regards experimentation with coalitions and the formation of elites and public policy networks that were now territorialized (Keating, 2005), without always shining when it came to the management of certain matters.[4] In Cardiff and Edinburgh, governments and parliament favored more social policies, less marked by New Labour's modernizing credo. The successive reforms in health, education, social services, or the universities sparked considerable resistance in the peripheral nations. The Scottish, for example, refused "top-up fees" (additional entrance fees for university). The Welsh deputies were highly mobilized on cultural issues; they gradually developed bilingualism and placed a whole set of agencies and partnerships under the control of the Assembly.

By contrast, the New Labour elites seem not to have clearly assimilated the dynamics of this system and its medium-term effects. The acceleration of New Labour reforms created opposition, especially in Scotland, which recalled the opposition to Margaret Thatcher's reforms in the 1980s. After an initial difficult period, the Scottish National Party soon had the wind in its sails again. It drew on the economic success of other small countries in Europe, particularly Ireland or Finland. Faced with this threat, the New Labour elites have thus far not known how to react, notwithstanding the involvement of Gordon Brown, who would be threatened were Scotland to demand independence. The Labour majority at Westminster crucially depends on Welsh and Scottish votes.

Following devolution, the territorial differentiation of parties, coalitions, electoral methods, institutions, and public policy tended to increase significantly, making the United Kingdom a rickety, asymmetrical system, evolving in a quasi-federal direction in the peripheries but massively centralized in England, where 85 percent of the population lives. Scotland remains in a peculiar situation, because per capita public expenditure there is around 20 percent higher than in England, this being financed by English taxpayers. The Scots consume around 10 percent more than they produce. The tensions are growing between Scots tempted by more autonomy, even independence, and the English, irritated at paying for their neighbors. The three hundredth anniversary of the Union (signed on 1 May 1707) was the occasion for an anti-Scottish campaign in England, and vice versa. Thus, during the regional elections of 1 May 2007, New Labour lost its majority in Wales and is now only the second party in Scotland. The Scottish nationalist leader Alex Salmond became first minister and leads a minority government. Political innovation via the "Celtic" periphery has induced further disruption in the traditional bipartisan balance of the United Kingdom and underscores the unfinished, insufficiently mature character of the reform of the union.

Northern Ireland: The Historic Personal Success of Tony Blair

The Irish question has been one of the most tragic subjects in British politics since the occupation of the island by the English. From the 1960s onward, conflicts between the Protestants of Ulster (the part of northern Ireland that remained in the United Kingdom after Irish independence in 1922), their paramilitaries, and the British police on the one hand, and the Catholics and the secret army of the Irish Republican Army (IRA) on the other, have fed an endless chronicle of communal hatreds, attacks, and assassinations—nearly four thousand dead in the last four decades.

Tony Blair and his secretaries of state (Mo Mowlam, then Peter Mandelson and Peter Hain) revived the peace process in Northern Ireland, by banking on the dynamic of devolution and offering the creation of a provincial parliament and government. The aim of the elections was to strengthen the moderate Catholic and Protestant parties, but the opposite happened: they were progressively marginalized in favor of the more radical parties of the two communities—Gerry Adams's and Martin McGuiness's Sinn Fein and the Reverend Ian Paisley's Ulster Democratic Party (UDP).

The first step was taken in 1998 with the Good Friday Agreement, which provided for an elected assembly of 108 members, an executive with fairly extensive powers (education, agriculture, health, economic development), and power-sharing between Protestants and Catholics. The two camps had to share the posts in the executive, particularly those of first minister and deputy first minister. This agreement owed a lot to Blair's activism and political leadership. He was personally involved in the negotiations. In order to persuade the Protestants, he brandished the threat of an agreement between London and Dublin to administer Ulster.

A first elected assembly and a government containing Protestants and Catholics operated for three years in an atmosphere of mutual suspicion, under the leadership of the Protestant David Trimble. But the Protestants remained very distrustful and the IRA was slow to implement unilateral disarmament, promised in exchange for the recruitment of Catholics to the Northern Irish police force. The peace process was interrupted in 2002, and the province was once again directly administered by the secretary of state for Northern Ireland. Through will-power and political courage, Blair secured a new agreement between the two camps in May 2007, illustrated by the historic handshake between the Protestant extremist Ian Paisley and the Sinn Fein leader Gerry Adams.

The peace process is still fragile, but the progress that has been made in ten years is considerable. Northern Irish society nevertheless remains extraordinarily divided between Catholics and Protestants. On the pretext of organizing a peaceful transition on the basis of concrete problems of government and public action, Blair has perhaps succeeded in establishing a lasting peace. If Tony Blair was able to leave 10 Downing Street with his head held high, his activity in behalf of peace in Ireland figured at the top of the balance sheet.

Reforming Local Government

In this area, as in others, the New Labour elites demonstrated a hyper-activism that destabilized existing actors and gradually led them to adapt to nonstop reforms.

Having consulted widely and organized debates, the principal ministers concerned, in particular Nick Rainsford (who served for a long period as minister for local communities and the regions) and the Deputy Prime Minister John Prescott (MP for Hull, working-class symbol of the government) put through a very complex law. It provided for the possibility of some local authorities choosing a way of appointing their executive and the possibility of an elected mayor—in particular, for the area of Greater London. In London, Ken Livingstone, elected as an independent, took the head of a pluralistic team containing Labour and Greens.[5] He then surprised everyone by applying a congestion charge to all cars entering the capital and involved himself in issues of economic development. The relative success of this experiment did not, however, persuade central government to increase his modest resources and powers. All consultation procedures on the limits, boundaries, and levels of local government underscored New Labour's preference for strictly supervised democratic participation.

In local government, resort to objectives and indicators proved particularly widespread. Basically, neither Blair nor Brown trusted elected officials, whom they suspected of defending public sector interests. The chancellor's promotion of the idea of "earned autonomy" might seem utterly ridiculous to anyone who takes the issues of local autonomy and democracy seriously. On the basis of synthetic indicators of "good" government developed by the Audit Office, the government rewarded good pupils by granting them a little more managerial autonomy and a little less inspection. Bad subjects, on the other hand, had to be punished and put back on the right track of good management à la New Labour (Le Galès, 2004).

The deputy prime minister, John Prescott, tried not only to further the interests of northern England but also to create an elected regional level of government. Unveiled in bombastic fashion, the "Northern Way" consisted in mobilizing priority resources, investment, and strategies for northern England. The not insignificant electoral stakes for Labour did not prevent the program's being aborted, because the commitments were not met. The creation of an elected regional assembly was demanded by elected representatives from the north-east (Newcastle) and north-west (Manchester and Liverpool), who felt constricted by comparison with their Scottish neighbors. But following a number of consultations, a minimalist proposal, which was complex and lacking resources, was put forward. Without any real political support from the government (apart from Prescott), it was massively rejected in a referendum and buried.

Ultimately, the debate on the creation of city-regions mobilized a good deal of energy and prompted numerous proposals for experimentation but led nowhere. There were two reasons for this failure: the regular change of ministers and the desire to create something that cost nothing, which essentially was useful for implementing new rationalizations, but did not possess any real power or a substantial budget—in short, a masquerade of local government.

Tony Blair and Gordon Brown foregrounded the theme of "new localism" as an antidote, so that they would not seem like ferocious centralizers. There was obviously no question of granting greater autonomy, powers, or resources to assemblies and executives elected at local and regional level. It was simply a matter of promoting the financial autonomy of basic units such as schools and hospitals in order to increase choices for consumers and pressures on service-providers via competition regulated by the central state.

In view of the incompletion of local government reform, the success of devolution seems an exception. New Labour does not like counterpowers or elected representatives. Britain is still the most centralized country in Western Europe.

Constitutional Reform: Tinkering in Progress

In their first term, New Labour energetically started work on renovating the unwritten Constitution, and this was to take up a good deal of the government's and Parliament's time. While fundamental alterations were made in constitutional arrangements, the reform dynamic exposed various contradictions, and a lack of interest and conviction on the part of Blair and his ministers. The main reforms passed were as follows:

- Adoption of a law on human rights in 1998 and—finally!—ratification of the European Convention on Human Rights. Because it codified intangible rights, this represented a major legal turning point. It provoked strong feelings on the part of the most conservative lawyers, alarmed by the abandonment of the tradition of civil liberties inscribed in the Magna Carta of 1215, in exchange for European rights ... for the protection of conditions of detention! New Labour thus clearly signaled its commitment to Europe and its desire to make Britain a *Rechtsstaat*—and not simply a state of common law that is adapted gradually and pragmatically.
- A law on freedom of information in 2000, eagerly awaited in a country where governments have long kept the essentials of their actions and decisions secret.
- The reorganization of Parliament's work and different reforms and reform initiatives concerning the House of Lords.
- Finally, in 2005, a constitutional reform rationalizing and reforming the justice system.

The Unfinished Reform of the House of Lords

Historically, Labour governments have only partly succeeded in transforming the unwritten Constitution of the United Kingdom (in the late 1960s, Wilson set in motion a significant reform that he was unable to see through). They have remained very loyal to the monarchy (and the influence of the aristocracy). They have proved incapable of protecting themselves against concentration of the media in the hands of a few big proprietors who, as a rule, are staunch supporters of the Conservatives. They have come up against the wall of money of the City of London and the powerful networks of the financial elite. They have failed with the House of Lords.

Let us recall that this anachronistic second parliamentary chamber was, until 1997, composed of around 1,200 lords, of whom a little over 750 were hereditary peers while approximately 350 were appointed (including the law lords, who form the country's highest legal instance, businessmen rewarded for services rendered, former ministers, and religious leaders). Obviously, the number of active members was much lower. The concentration of heirs of the aristocracy on the one hand, and representatives of interests and members appointed by the government on the other, helped preserve a form of official clientelism that approximated to corruption. The House of Lords was the most antidemocratic, the most reactionary, and the most conservative body in all of the Western democracies (Crewe, 2005). Containing very few women, and few or no members of minorities, it represented the old British elite. During hard-fought debates in the House of Commons, the Conservatives had no hesitation mobilizing those who were dubbed the "backwoodsmen." These aristocrats, who were often big landowners, came to vote only on major occasions, particularly against new taxes, on the issue of joining Europe, to defend the vestiges of empire (like Rhodesia in the 1960s), or when their privileges were at stake.

Consequently, some hoped for a radical reform from the Blair government. It was not inactive. Major figures in the government like Lord Irvine, Robin Cook, and then Jack Straw made proposals, convened many committees, and organized votes. On this issue the government sought gradual change and consensus, while controlling the process and exploiting its short-term advantage. The debate occupied minds from 1997, finally giving rise to some half-measures (Russell, 2000). While the government succeeded in abolishing the majority of hereditary members, it could not resolve to establish an elected second chamber.[6] New Labour's preference was for a chamber composed largely of appointed members—and, with the passage of time, members appointed by them. The imbroglio created by these debates was rather exceptional (Norton, 2005). Tony Blair always favored a second chamber of appointed members, albeit with revision of the appointments procedure, whereas others, including within the government, tried to negotiate a percentage of elected lords (20 percent, 30 percent, a majority). It was not until the beginning of 2007 that the House of Commons finally proposed a reform of the House of Lords that contained neither members appointed by the government, nor heirs of the nobility.[7] Reform is on the agenda of Blair's successor. The conduct of these debates by the government was a symbol neither of clarity over principles or the direction of the reform, nor of political courage. Mentor of Blair and lord chancellor, Lord Irvine justified himself by resorting to the pragmatic genius of the nation (!): "[T]he strands do not spring from a single master plan, however much that concept might appeal to purists. We prefer the empirical genius of our nation: to go, pragmatically, step by step, for change through continuing consent. Principled steps, not absolutist master plans, are the winning route to constitutional renewal in unity and in peace" (cited by Flinders, 2006: 121).

Neville Johnson, a skeptical Conservative who is professor of politics at Oxford, interpreted this in less charitable terms. According to him, the British Constitution is above all "a collection of practices, sanctioned by law, political judgement and prevailing habits, that is understood by the participants in them as summarising the permissible way of governing the country." Thus, "the tale of efforts to reform the composition of the Lords since the passage of the House of Lords Act 1999 is basically one of hesitant starts, muddled outcomes, and continued adaptation of existing conventions and practices to meet the convenience of the ruling politicians" (Johnson, 2004: 171). In other words, the government gave the impression of playing it by ear, in accordance with its short-term interests. Supporters of more radical reform within the party or government were not supported by the leadership, which let slip a major opportunity to democratize institutions.

As regards the House of Commons, the New Labour leadership, when it was in opposition, had stated loud and clear its intention to do away with secrecy and the marginalization of Parliament. It had insisted on the need to make government more accountable. After 2001, Robin Cook carried through a series of adaptations of Parliament's modus operandi (especially the hours and timetable of sessions and sittings) and in particular made possible a strengthening of select committees.[8] Specialist committees of the House of Commons, whether permanent or not, as well as special committees of inquiry thus obtained additional resources. For the first time in decades, the prime minister agreed to reply to questions from one of these committees. Overall, the balance sheet is not brilliant, but it is significant. The conditions of parliamentary work, and its ability to control the executive, have been improved.

The Constitutional Reform of 2005

Tony Blair had no hesitation in running the risk of being accused of nepotism when he used his discretionary powers of appointment to the House of Lords to appoint various intimates to his government.[9] From 2003 the new lord chancellor, Lord Falconer, mobilized the principles of democratization of the political system and modernization to propose a set of rather innovative reforms whose future remains in doubt. Denouncing the archaism of the legal system, New Labour proposed to abolish the post of lord chancellor, who enjoyed the peculiarity of being a member of the government, presiding over the House of Lords (and hence being in Parliament), and being head of the legal system. A prime example of a total confusion of powers! New Labour also suggested the creation of a Supreme Court, a committee for appointing judges, and a Department of Constitutional Affairs (combining the Justice Department and oversight of Scottish and Welsh affairs).

This project, which marked completion of New Labour's program for renovating a constitution that is no longer really unwritten (people no longer dared speak of "modernization" in 2005, because by then the term was universally rejected) was sharply criticized. Opponents suspected the government of wanting to reduce the trend toward increasing judicial power in the political sphere. For several years, in fact, judges, opposing the government, denounced the authoritarian drift of successive home secretaries (David Blunkett, then Charles Clarke and John Reid)—or cast doubt on the policies of openness of information. In addition, the changes proposed preserved the Westminster model (that is, centralization around Parliament and the government). They consolidated the domination of the House of Commons (and, de facto, that of the government) without creating a Supreme Court equipped with powers equivalent to those of courts or councils in other democracies. The law finally passed in 2005 was the result of an ambiguous compromise, because the office of lord chancellor was not abolished in the end (but profoundly altered), and the powers of the new bodies were not really clarified. After many debates, the creation of the Department of Justice still encountered a great deal of opposition from judges who did not obtain the guarantees of independence they had asked for.

Proportional Representation with Reluctance

Mobilized with the Liberal Democrats against the Conservatives, New Labour, once elected, hesitated to change the voting system, keystone of the British political system. As always on these issues, the Labour Party's attitude toward the introduction of proportional representation fluctuated with its position in the system. Hostile to it after the war, Labour took an interest in it after 1979 and supported it following their defeat in 1992. However, divisions persisted at the top of the party between those who regarded such a reform as a way of ensuring the lasting domination of the center-left (albeit at the price of alliances), and those who balked at questioning the majority system. Secret agreements had been made between the Liberal Democrat leader Paddy Ashdown and Tony Blair. The Liberal Democrats hoped that a narrow majority in the Commons would allow them to take part in a coalition government. The overwhelming majority obtained in 1997 soon eliminated that possibility. Tony Blair, who had never publicly committed himself on the question, made do with charging a parliamentary committee to make proposals for general elections. Published in 1998, these remained a dead letter, and the promised referendum was indefinitely postponed. Use of a mixed system in the peripheral nations, and the need to form a coalition with the Liberal Democrats, doubtless increased New Labour's appreciation of the undivided power that it enjoyed at Westminster and strengthened its conviction that the common good was best served by enlightened and effective majority governments (Faucher, 2000).

The "Europeanization" of British Politics?

In 1997, New Labour came to power with a positive attitude toward the European Union and its relationship with the UK that contrasted with the resistance and acrimony that had characterized the Thatcher and Major governments. This was made possible by the emergence of a new consensus within the Labour elites. While the left had been opposed to joining a European Community, attitudes changed during the 1980s. First, European social policies appeared as a means to undermine Thatcher's neoliberal reforms. A new generation of Labour MPs, elected from 1983, warmed up to the European project and contributed to impose a new orthodoxy within the party (Baker and Seawright, 1998). As New Labour accepted the legacy of Thatcher, it no longer opposed institutions initially viewed as antithetical to the social democratic project (Hay, 1999). New Labour's consensus[10] on Europe allowed it to reap the benefits of the damage the issue inflicted on its main rival, while postponing any decision on membership of the Eurozone.[11]

The first few years in government presented a marked contrast with the Conservatives: New Labour signed the Social Charter and the prime minister led the initiative for closer cooperation with the two main European partners, France and Germany,[12] before developing deeper bilateral relations with other countries, such as Spain and Belgium. After the six months of the UK presidency of the European Union in 1998, Tony Blair requested a review of the role of his country in the union in order to identify areas in which it was possible to take a more proactive role so that the process of Europeanization could entail not only British adaptation to European initiatives but also the uploading of policy approaches and vision to the European level. Great efforts were deployed to integrate the European constraints and challenges into the British system of government. The Cabinet Office European secretary doubled its staff and effectively coordinated the governmental approach to all EU-related policies and issues. Its proactive role was helped by the new style of government and the concentration of power in the hands of the prime minister. No longer passive or contrarian on the European scene, the New Labour governments projected their own vision of the EU while adapting reflexively. It notably encouraged all departments to develop their own relationships with Brussels, and the Foreign Office itself created new positions both in London and in the Belgium capital. Only the Treasury remained on the sidelines, guarding jealously not only the criteria it had itself imposed as preconditions for joining the Eurozone but also the prerogatives of the chancellor over all economic matters. By 2004 the Europeanization efforts were deemed successful, and the program was slowed down (Bulmer and Burch, 2006). There is no doubt that, as Tony Blair left office in June 2007, his country was demonstrably more integrated with its Continental counterparts economically, culturally, as well as ideationally.

Such changes in approach were indeed remarkable and justify in themselves the impression, broadly shared across Europe, of Tony Blair as a fervent European. However, it is also important to underline continuities. Two need to be addressed. Strong economic ties with the Commonwealth have in the past justified resistance to economic integration and in particular to the Common Agricultural Policy. More important, any further engagements with European partners on defense or on foreign policy (Leruez, 2005: 105) are circumscribed by the "special relationship" with the United States.[13] During the Blair years, there is no better example than the determination of Tony Blair to go to war in Iraq (Danchev, 2007), despite the opposition of France and Germany and at the risk of endangering Britain's newly established European credentials.[14]

The transformation of the UK in relation to the EU can be seen as a dialogical process of Europeanization of British politics and Anglicization of the union. On the one hand, many of the constitutional changes taking place in the UK, and in particular the challenge to the centralization of the British polity through the emergence, beyond Westminster, of multilevel governance, took place against a background of increased integration within the EU. Despite its poor reputation, the UK has been one of the most diligent countries in the translation of European directives into national legislation. The third sector and the powerful lobbying industry have also increasingly turned to Brussels (Chapman, 2005), where they have benefited from their longer established tradition of lobbying. The electoral system has often been seen as a crucial anchor for the British political system in that it has largely contributed to preserve the two-party system at Westminster. Although nothing has changed as far as the House of Commons is concerned, the first-past-the-post system has given way to proportional representation for elections to the European Parliament and regional assemblies.[15]

On the other hand, one can argue that the Europeanization of the UK is a subtle trade-off as Europe itself has ideationally adapted. The British position had long been particularly favorable to the economic dimension of the union, and the construction of the single market fit with such long-term priorities. Although it remains outside of the Eurozone, the UK has by and large abided by the convergence criteria in line with its economic policy orientations. Moreover, the European Union agenda matches neatly some of the British concerns. Budgetary reform, for instance, was a long-term priority. European policies on competition and transparency through target settings and evaluation of performance echoed UK domestic policies.[16] In 2001, the Lisbon agenda focused European efforts on creating "the most dynamic and competitive knowledge-based economy" fit for the challenges of economic globalization; it was also particularly resonant with New Labour's obsession with globalization and modernization. Not only had the domestic and economic successes of New Labour impressed abroad but the charm offensive and search for compromise have borne fruit. During the first mandate in particular, the UK came out of its isolation. In Nice in 2001, the UK accepted the extension of qualified majority voting to thirty new areas, and Tony Blair successfully argued to his compatriots that this would increase the UK's influence (as it restricted the veto powers of other member states on issues promoted by the UK). Enlargement further strengthened the British position, as the new rules meant that it could henceforth find allies in southern or in the "New" Europe against proposals promoted by the traditional Franco-German couple.[17] In 2004, Blair successfully worked for the selection of Manuel Barroso as president of the commission against the Belgium prime minister supported by France and Germany.

Tony Blair presented himself as committed to reconciling the British public and British politics with the European Union, but he may have been more convincing to European leaders than to his own compatriots. Despite the divisions caused by his decision to support the United States in the war in Iraq, Blair was still considered in 2007 as a serious contender for the position of president of Europe created by the Lisbon Treaty. Unfortunately, the rejection of the treaty by the Irish in June 2008 further postponed such a consecration of his career.[18] On the home front, Tony Blair has been less convincing. New Labour never engaged public opinion nor campaigned actively to cement the UK's position in Europe. The adoption of the euro was very early on depoliticized. Although there was a commitment to joining, the decision was postponed to the Greek calends and the satisfaction of the chancellor's five economic tests.[19] Such conditions emphasized technical criteria for membership, thereby diffusing the political dimension of any such move. In 2003, the assessment concluded that the criteria were not successfully met, and any debate on the euro was ruled out until after the next general election. The skeptical Iron Chancellor, already at the head of the least cooperative department, thus retained close control over the British economy, centralizing power until the day he would become prime minister. Attention was further deflected in the following years by enlargement and the ratification process for the European Constitution. While domestic pressures forced Blair to promise a referendum on the treaty, the campaign was postponed after the next general election. Such delay proved an excellent bet, as the defeat of the referendums in France and The Netherlands allowed the Labour government never to have to face the arduous task of campaigning for it.

Centralization of the Executive

Blair as president or Gordon Brown as master of the universe? While constitutional reform betrayed a chaotic, unguided process, rationalization of the executive indicated the priority given to strengthening the executive's piloting and control capacities. New Labour's activist state required administrative capacities and advisors mobilized for the government's projects. Blair and Brown therefore strengthened their offices and their administration, following the example of what is seen in most Western democracies.

Traditionally, British government is presented as cabinet government. The British prime minister's civil servants (Cabinet Office) dispose of very few resources, because he or she is regarded as primus inter pares, first among equals. By contrast, each minister has a sizable body of civil servants and great autonomy. Coordination is conducted by the mandarins of the Civil Service, within the "Whitehall village."[20]

While the Labour Party long preserved a polycephalous form of organization, in order to limit the concentration of power in the leader's hands, the period of Blair's leadership was characterized by a concentration of power in Downing Street. These developments had begun under Margaret

Thatcher, but had been interrupted by John Major, who had sought to govern in a more consensual fashion despite the tensions within his team. Tony Blair accepted the Thatcherite legacy and pursued its logic up to the fall of 2006. Shortly after he had been obliged to announce his departure, Tony Blair suddenly announced a return to "cabinet government." This turn can be interpreted as an attempt to consolidate his legacy and nibble away in advance at the powers of his rival and successor, Gordon Brown.

Following Margaret Thatcher, Tony Blair significantly strengthened the Cabinet Office's strategic and coordinating powers. In 2001 the Private Office and the Policy Unit were fused under the direction of Jonathan Powell, who served as head of the prime minister's office. The number of special advisors doubled. Three new directorates were created: the Delivery Unit (specializing in monitoring the delivery of policy); the Office of Public Services Reform (the office responsible for monitoring reorganization of the public sector); and the Strategy Unit (the unit responsible for strategic thinking about government action). Each of these organizations was composed of a small team of senior civil servants, political advisors, consultants, and experts. Tony Blair thus equipped himself with a real personal staff. Margaret Thatcher had broken new ground by opening access to important posts in her cabinet or in departments to major employers or consultants. The aim was to reflect on the conditions for policy delivery, in order to identify solutions outside the traditional models proposed by the civil service.

Here we find the mixture of voluntarism, pragmatism about means, and micromanagement characteristic of the Blair-Brown governments.[21] Blair strengthened links with think tanks, groups of academics, heads of community associations, and groups of entrepreneurs, in order to mobilize new ideas and new projects. Advisors intervened in policy, and the civil service was reconfigured to produce results and coordinate public action. In the process, the civil service underwent significant expansion, with an increase of around 20 percent (100,000 people) in ten years of New Labour government. To defuse criticisms of the creeping state control of British society in anticipation of the next elections, in 2006 Gordon Brown launched an economy plan that aimed to abolish or transfer 100,000 jobs in the civil service (with a percentage being set for redeployment in agencies or at the local and regional level).

Several factors, including the style of the Blair government and the life-style of 10 Downing Street,[22] fueled commentaries evoking a "presidential-ization" of British government (Foley, 2004):

- longevity in government (ten years) and the legitimacy afforded by three successive electoral victories.
- Blair dominated his government and British political life. Moreover, he clearly downgraded the role of cabinet meetings and eroded the principle of government collegiality, in favor of regular, face-to-face interaction with different ministers in his office. Hence the formula of "government by sofa."
- the personalization of politics marginalized other actors.
- highly disciplined parties lost their central role in British democracy, while Parliament was bypassed in favor of direct communication in the media.

This interpretation nevertheless comes up against the role and political in-fluence of Gordon Brown. This led journalists to mock the "turbulent dual monarchy of Brown and Blair" giving instructions to other ministers.[23] The two men worked with success—sometimes in concert, sometimes against each other—to strengthen the strategic capacities of the Cabinet Office (prime minister) and the Treasury.

The strength of British government lies in control of a majority in Par-liament. The existence of disciplined parties and a two-party system gener-ally ensure that the victorious party can implement policy projects without any real interference from the opposition, which is essentially reduced to the role of goad and verbal criticism during lively sessions of questions to the government. Parliament's sovereignty and authority have been attacked on many fronts: European integration, devolution, increase in executive power, strengthened party discipline. These developments began before New Labour's arrival in power, but the trends became more marked. Con-trol of the government by parliamentary committees was limited by the lack of convincing opposition from the Conservatives, who were exhausted and divided. In some cases, the role of goad fell to Labour rebels. Thus, two committees of inquiry, respectively chaired by Lords Hutton and Butler, tried to uncover the decision-making circuits that led to Britain's engagement in Iraq (independently of the fact that the decision in principle had been taken very much earlier). They did not really succeed in uncovering the machinery of government, but did demonstrate that the prime minister had not respected the traditional modus operandi. Instead, he relied on a narrow network of advisors and collaborators, thus short-circuiting Parliament, the civil service, and even the heads of the military as regards Iraq.[24]

Communications and Rationalization of the Executive

The organization of ubiquitous, strategic government communications has led to Parliament's being sidelined in debates. The prime minister reserved for himself not only the last word on decisions but also the political initiative and media impact. Thatcher had developed the government's communications unit with the aid of her advisor, Harvey Thomas. Under Blair's leadership, his team of political advisors and communications representatives became the nerve center of government. The autonomy of the Labour Party and departments of state in communications was reduced; the role of senior civil servants was limited in favor of consultants. The Blair team's concern with control of the political agenda led, in practice, to withdrawing priority from the House of Commons when it came to political announcements, which were now invariably made directly to the press. But this did not prevent lively parliamentary debates. Blair participated in Commons debates only once a week, for the televised session of Prime Minister's Questions. On the other hand, he took part once a month in questions from the press—something that was presented as proof of accountability.[25]

Tony Blair never hesitated to put himself on the line for significant reforms. He took risks, committed himself, swept resistance aside, and communicated nonstop with the public. This activism sometimes occurred at the expense of more structural reforms. The assumption of control over government bodies by New Labour networks became more marked over the years, replacing the Conservative elites. Tony Blair also favored diversity in recruitment, the arrival of personnel from the world of business, sometimes from charity organizations, who were appointed to government (after ennoblement) or placed in responsible positions in numerous agencies (BBC, British Council, regulatory authorities, the Arts Council, and others). This tendency conveyed an enthusiasm for the enterprise model and its gradual imposition on the British political scene. The language of business was accepted as the language of modernity and success. Slogans such as "UK plc,"[26] or "Britain is open for business," multiplied. Official documents comparing government departments with the boardrooms of firms, or teachers with the managers of branch offices, became routine.

Furthermore, departmental organization was subject to alteration and reconstruction, in line with the logic of rationalization or the political influence of some particular minister, as in the case of John Prescott, deputy prime minister. As was frequently the case with New Labour reforms, rigorous principles of streamlined action and pursuit of efficiency were coupled with high-profile media presentation and hyperinnovation with sometimes dubious effects. Thus, John Prescott was in charge of a super-Department of Transport, the Environment, Relations with local authorities and the regions, Housing, and so on, which was fairly rapidly dismantled. The makeup of the Blair governments reveals this impatience, this desire for nonstop change. The division of duties between departments and appointments was constantly revised in short order. Following Margaret Thatcher, Blair employed a considerable number of ministers. Loyalists like John Reid became famous for their changes of portfolio, sometimes in the course of the same year. Various agencies and roles (for example, antidrug czar) were created for their media impact. They clearly answered to the need for legitimacy through incessant action. But the concern with communicating policy effectively sometimes impaired the coherence of government action or the effectiveness of its delivery. All government ministers were led to enroll in this dynamic of modernization and to exist by announcements, draft reforms, and new performance indicators. Government heavyweights like David Blunkett, Charles Clarke, and John Reid (all three of them education secretary and then home secretary), Patricia Hewitt (secretary of state for

Trade and Industry and then for Health), and Alistair Darling (Transport) thus developed their own agenda and multiplied initiatives.

The prime minister's action also depends on his ability to control his parliamentary majority. The government's omnipotence was enhanced by the discipline of MPs. Blair had to accommodate the party's tendencies, including part of the left that was hostile to him, or indeed supporters of Gordon Brown; and he proved capable of doing so. He used all the resources available to the leadership: promotion within the government, the party, or parliamentary committees; sanctions, promises, threats, calumny, press leaks, or negotiations on some particular point. Despite the existence of a substantial number of dissidents, the majorities obtained in 1997 and 2001 were sufficient to guarantee control of the agenda. Over the course of ten years, Blair faced several parliamentary rebellions, particularly on the issues of university fees and health reforms. On several occasions, his majority was reduced to a handful of MPs (Cowley, 2005). However, it was not until November 2005 that we witnessed the prime minister's first defeat in the House of Commons, in a vote on the period of detention of terrorist suspects. The success of this rebellion was indicative of the prime minister's politically weakened condition.

Critics and some biographers of Blair stress the extent to which he had to arrive at accommodations during his first term. Lacking any experience of power, he had to learn to master the machinery of government and its administration (Seldon, 2004). This was made possible by a functional division of labor with Gordon Brown, master in the micromanagement of government action. Blair and his advisors were formed in politics on the opposition benches, in the media, and the working groups of think tanks. In this framework Tony Blair always excelled at the art of persuasion, at putting a programmatic innovation in perspective. He was brilliant in this key dimension of political work, constantly under media pressure. By contrast, he had no particular contacts with what, by its very nature, is the slower world of public policy. But there too New Labour learned the lessons of Margaret Thatcher on the importance of the presentation of decisions, actions, and outcomes. It hit upon the mobilizing slogans that destabilized vested interests and actors, without necessarily making it possible to achieve the anticipated results. The recourse to external consultants was symptomatic of the search for new ideas, sometimes given priority over reality or the pace of change.

The image of Gordon Brown was a counterpoint to that of Tony Blair as president, and one can not isolate the legacy of Blair from the key role played by his chancellor over the course of ten years.[27] His longevity and success in managing the economy gave him unquestioned authority. From the moment he arrived, he strove to control public expenditure by systematizing the instruments of control introduced by the Conservatives. Having accepted their rigid public spending framework at the outset, he developed the Comprehensive Spending Review—that is, the systematic, planned analysis of expenditure by departments and then by agencies. These analyses were carried out over three-year cycles in order to facilitate forecasts of the deficit, borrowing, and margins for investment. Gradually, these exercises became more precise and were combined with targets for reducing costs and improving performance. At the Treasury Brown set up specialist groups for monitoring the expenditure of each of the other departments. Thanks to the systematic development of information management, Brown and his team obtained a detailed knowledge of the resources and capacities of other departments and agencies, and an unrivaled expertise in the art of piloting change on the basis of altering targets. By defining the rules of the game of public policy, and by regularly altering targets and indicators, they were able to destabilize the others. The iron financial discipline they imposed transformed senior civil servants and agency heads into managers, judged predominantly on the meeting of their budget and objectives.

Like Blair, Brown strengthened the strategic powers of the exchequer to the point where he gradually acquired control of the delivery of public policy thanks to financial indicators. Also like Blair, Brown enhanced the role of his special advisors and cultivated links with think tanks, while working closely with groups of academics and experts on particular subjects. He too shook up the traditional civil service by introducing brilliant young economists or strengthening the role of regulatory authorities. Leadership of these agencies was often given to academics—something that created conflicts with departmental heads. Brown used to the full the margin for maneuver given him by the prime minister in their initial governmental pact. Via the budget, he ensured the coherence and the promotion of a large number of reforms—to the point of sometimes seeming like the man in the shadows pulling all the strings of government. Given Blair's political weight, this image was obviously exaggerated. On the other hand, the control Brown exercised occasionally blocked the delivery of reforms, and he attracted the wrath of other ministers, who sometimes characterized his methods as brutal Stalinism.

The government's objective was to modernize institutions, democratize them, make them open and transparent; to prioritize honesty so as to restore the confidence of the British people in the political system. At the end of the period, what was achieved is considerable, but the outcomes are very mixed. Centralization, hyperactivism, and concern for control were accompanied by an important process of devolution and democratization of certain bodies. The reforms in the direction of openness tended to be passed during the first term. With the passage of time, centralization became the government's dominant feature.

Renewal of the Constitution is a work in progress that does not seem to be following any very clear logic. Devolution launched a movement of renewal of British politics and a reorganization of public action, which has not yet been stabilized. In a sense, the Blair government opened the way to what is becoming a polycentric model of government that has been adopted by others in Europe. Centralization of executive resources and capacities is not in itself altogether surprising, for it is often a necessary condition for avoiding the collapse of reforms. By contrast, hyperactivism and the stress on communications certainly made it possible to destabilize the agents of public action and traditional bodies like Parliament or the senior civil service—but also generated problematic effects for the delivery of public action and mobilization, and the association of concerned groups, as well as for control of the executive by Parliament.

4   The Reinvention of the Labour Party: "New Labour, New Britain"

Parties that do not change die, and this party is a living movement not a historical monument.

—Tony Blair, Labour Party Conference, 1994

In 1992 Neil Kinnock narrowly lost to Margaret Thatcher's successor, John Major. This fourth defeat (following Labour's electoral disasters in 1983 and 1987) led observers to wonder whether Conservative domination might be interminable (Jowell et al., 1994; Heath et al., 2001). During the 1980s, an internal debate on the left of the party had opposed modernizers to those who awaited the collapse of the Thatcher governments. The former made a significant contribution to a renewal of analyses of power, multicultural-ism, and capitalism. Having understood the extent to which Thatcherite strategy was a response to the transformation of the British economy and globalization, they sought to develop a Labour response to "New Times."[1] For them, returning to the past was no longer an option. The premature death of the leader John Smith in 1994 made possible the rapid emergence of young leaders.

When Tony Blair was elected leader of the Labour Party in 1994, the activists were ready to accept unprecedented political changes in order to win back power. The young leader exploited this inner-party atmosphere to embark at once upon a program of "modernization" of the party that involved a host of measures, ranging from the symbolic (rewriting clause 4 of the constitution,[2] and accepting the market model), to the mediatic (adoption of a new name: New Labour), the political (a promise to observe the constraints of the Conservative budget and not raise taxes), and the organizational (reform of discussion procedures and centralization of membership services). Tony Blair, Gordon Brown, and their teams had one idea in mind: to prepare for the return to power and a medium-term strategy for government. These new leaders had virtually no nostalgia for the great working-class movement that was Labour. They wanted to modernize the party, modernize the country, and seize the opportunities offered by the new era to win elections and govern. A number of these changes were based on reforms introduced after 1983 by Kinnock and Smith, but what was new was that the forces of New Labour also changed the party's internal culture and image.

For them, the party served as an experimental terrain. The internal reforms were comparable to those subsequently introduced in the country by the Blair governments: distancing from the trade unions in favor of think thanks and communications experts; stressing the individual; reforming policy-making procedures; and introducing the logics of management and audit. Political leadership was important: changes in form, procedure, and policy orientation altered the expectations, interests, and participation of activists, at the cost of tensions inside the party.

The rhetoric of novelty, constantly harped on by the leadership, was adopted by the media and gradually naturalized. It depicted the representatives of New Labour as modernizing heroes wrestling with conservative forces attached to outdated privileges and reluctant to seize the opportunities offered by the new age that was dawning. It reinforced the commitment to the effect that "elected as New Labour, we shall govern as New Labour."[3] The aim in creating a new Labour Party—New Labour—was to symbolize the transformation of the old party so as to win over the electorate and reassure the Conservative media. The oppositions between the modern and the archaic, progress and the status quo, the democratic and the bureaucratic, were used to facilitate and justify the changes and delegitimate currents of resistance, especially from the left of the party. Protest by activists played a crucial role in the strategy, because it gave credibility to the opposition between "old" and "new" Labour projected by the "modernizers" as the decisive internal cleavage (Faucher-King, 2005: 60–61). The Blair team constantly invoked the need for government to overcome the inertial tendencies of those who opposed an inevitable modernization. Internal resistance thus also served to promote the image of a radical, triumphant leadership. However, surveys of members indicate that from 1999 onward there was no longer any significant ideological difference between new members and activists (Seyd and Whiteley, 2002).

The forces of New Labour were concerned to control their image and interpretations of their actions and policies, in order to demonstrate that the transformation of the party was not a cosmetic exercise but reflected a profound change. Such an approach was no doubt inspired by marketing considerations—in other words, an organization is more effective when the employees (in this instance, the activists) who apply its objectives adhere to the aims and values professed by the collective. Consequently, it was important for the forces of New Labour to ensure that the party's base had assimilated the transmutation of the old into the new presented in the media. The party's modernization was no easy task, and the New Labour elites would not have enjoyed a consensus on objectives and principles and trade union support were it not for the exceptional historical conditions. By 2007 the party had been emptied of its capacities for intermediation with society and, in the space of ten years, lost half its membership.[4] But it had become a formidable machine for winning elections.[5]

Loosening the Links with the Trade Unions

Founded in 1900 to represent the interests of the working class, the Labour Party maintained close links with the trade unions throughout the twentieth century. Individual members were accepted only from 1918 onward. From the trade union tradition Labour's party culture derived an ambivalent relationship with money (which resulted in prudent financial administration and heavy dependence on the unions as a source of funding), a recurrent fear of betrayal by the elites (hence a belated institutionalization of leadership positions and a polycephalous organization), and finally a profound identification with, and loyalty to, the working-class movement. The unions supplied the elected leaders not only with regular funding but also with a certain stability in the face of pressure from activists. Once the more leftist period of the 1970s was over, they resumed their role as supporters of the Labour leadership.[6]

The unions changed profoundly during the Conservative years. Some (like the TGWU) remained close to traditional values, while others developed in a public sector subject to government pressure, and numerous unions amalgamated or changed their name. The leader of the Trade Union Congress (TUC), John Monks, was a moderate acutely aware of the need to advance the unions and the party.[7] Some leaders joined the teams of Tony Blair and Gordon Brown, or performed duties within the Labour Party. They developed close links with their members. They were also conscious of having emerged from their prolonged confrontation with the Thatcher governments weakened and delegitimated. The press depicted them as reactionary, archaic, undemocratic forces. The election of a Labour government, by definition less hostile to their cause than the Conservatives, was one of their priorities. Consequently, they were ready to make concessions. After the 1992 defeat they agreed to a reduction in their influence at the annual party conference from 90 percent to 70 percent, and then to 50 percent when the number of individual members reached 300,000.[8] They renounced the bloc vote, which allowed the largest of them to exercise considerable influence on decisions. They also promised to consult their members before their leaders adopted a position and cast their votes in the party. In 1994, when they accounted for only one-third of the votes in the composition of the electoral college for choosing the leader (and selecting candidates), they supported Tony Blair.

However, New Labour's leadership was convinced of the need to accept a globalized capitalism and join forces with the middle classes, who were often hostile to the unions. Blair immediately announced that his government would not engage in favoritism and would treat unions and business organizations identically. These declarations did not stop the unions and the party from continuing their collaboration. Once in government, and notwithstanding the weakening of the liaison committee, the largest unions retained access to members of the government and their ability to construct important voting coalitions in internal bodies. In exchange for concessions obtained behind the scenes, they gave the leadership stabilizing support, but the slightest dependence of the government on them allowed them to express themselves more freely.

Once in charge of the country, Blair and his ministers shamelessly used the unions as sources of legitimation. They served as a foil in the modernizing rhetoric, and the government regularly denounced them in public as conservative forces opposed to the country's modernization. Yet at the same time they provided loyal support and activists. Inside the party, the forces of New Labour often relied on the votes of the big union federations in important decisions by the National Executive Committee, the Policy Forum, or at conference (for example, to avoid a defeat on Iraq at the 2002 conference, or to prevent certain issues featuring on the conference agenda), or to secure the selection of modernizing candidates in key constituencies.[9]

Nevertheless, systematic support for business or the introduction of market mechanisms and indicators in the areas of health and education provoked open conflicts with public-sector unions. Disagreements centered in particular on the way in which the government sought to raise the productivity of public services by introducing procedures and practices from the private sector, challenging the existing culture and systems. Blair and his team presented themselves as champions of the general interest (that of the consumers of public services, defended by the government) against the (particular) interests of public-sector workers (defended by the unions). On such occasions, individual members were given priority (particularly during public debates at the party conference) as a prop for the leadership against backward-looking, and sometimes divided, unions.

Continuing political disagreements, and accusations against the unions by the government, contributed to a radicalization of some of them and to the election of left-wing leaders of the two largest unions (TGWU and GMB, Britain's General Union) in 2003. Finally, the FBU (Fire Brigades Union) disaffiliated from the party, allowing its local branches to support different political parties. Nevertheless, despite violent conflicts and attacks, the organizational links have not been broken, and the unions remain actors who cannot be ignored in inner-party negotiations. They played a crucial role in the adoption of internal reforms, resisting any erosion of their role but facilitating the dilution of the power of activists. Certainly, the

TABLE 2

The Main Trade Unions (figures from the TUC, April 2007)

Acronym	Full name	Members	General Secretary	Sector of activities
ICEM	International Federation of Chemical Energy, Mine and General Workers Union	2,000,000	Tony Woodley and Derek Simpson, cosecretaries	Merger of Amicus and Transport and General Workers Union (TGWU) in March 2007
Unison	Trade Union for People Delivering Public Services	1,317,000	Dave Prentis	Public services and public sector union
GMB	Britain's General Union	575,370	Paul Kenny	General trade union including, in particular, public sector and public works
USDAW	Union of Shop, Distributive and Allied Workers	340,653	John Hannett	General trade union for employees in the sector of distribution, food production, and services
PCS	Public and Commercial Services Union	312,725	Mark Serwotka	General trade union including the public sector and public agencies, services connected with information
NUT	National Union of Teachers	254,862	Steve Sinnott	Teachers and education sector

liaison committee with the unions has not always been maintained at its highest level of activity, but overall it remains advantageous to the unions to support a Labour government, even an unsatisfactory one, rather than risk the return of the Conservatives.

Promoting a Direct Relationship with Members

While the party-union link was preserved, the New Labour leadership essentially promoted individual members—a policy initiated by Neil Kinnock in the 1980s to oppose the most left-wing activists. Breaking with the tradition of the working-class movement, from the 1990s onward the party adopted an important number of reforms tending toward direct participation by members. The initial results of votes using the individual, direct suffrage of members at the beginning of the 1990s made it possible for the modernizers to eject the left from the National Executive Committee.[10] The group that took power with Blair soon came to see this procedure as a way of freeing itself from the unions (archaic) and the activists (too radical) alike.

The dynamic instilled by the leadership of Tony Blair in the New Labour Party, and the rejection of a catastrophic Conservative government, were powerful mobilizing factors from the standpoint of the 1997 general election. New Labour launched a vast recruitment campaign with new marketing methods, aiming to attract managers and members of the liberal professions and of the middle and upper classes from outside traditional Labour networks. They simplified procedures for joining, thanks to the centralization of applications (it was no longer necessary to go through a local section), the creation of a national membership list, and the use of payment facilities (especially debit and credit cards). They also created new incentives for joining: new members had the right to vote during internal elections for the leader and for party posts, as well as for the selection of candidates; they also had a right to information thanks to the creation of personalized mail and magazines for members. Finally, they enjoyed a new right to participate in forums presented as a way of contributing directly to policy formation. These "rights" received abundant publicity and were presented as proof of the party's democratization. In truth they represented very little in the way of concessions, but in practice they were perceived by activists as a dilution of their (already meager) influence.

To begin with, the recruitment strategy was effective. It made it possible to abandon reliance on the working-class family and accelerated the break with a trade union culture characterized by activist contact, local anchorage, sociability, and identification with a tradition—a culture that was in the process of disappearing in the Britain of the 1990s, especially in the south of the country. The new recruits were barely encouraged to make contact with the existing local sections, out of a fear that they would be put off or, alternatively, "contaminated" by the archaisms and the jargon of Old Labour activists. The party no longer presented itself as a family, but as a professionalized organization where services were exchanged and opportunities offered.

In 1995 the number of members exceeded 300,000, bringing about a significant alteration in the political balance within the party. Union influence at conference was reduced to 50 percent. Consequently, delegates of the individual membership acquired a crucial role at the annual conference, and they increased the unpredictability of decisions, because they formed a less disciplined group than the trade unionists. Bound by a loosely prescriptive mandate from their local group, they were that much more susceptible to being influenced by speakers. In response, the leadership strengthened its control over debates. Far removed from the shouting matches of the 1980s, they sometimes became bland. At the same time, a new rule of parity for selecting delegates altered the makeup of conference and the governing bodies by substantially increasing the role of women. It also established the rotation of delegation by preventing the most battle-hardened activists from returning each year. Blair's team hoped that inexperienced delegates and women would change both the image of the party and the atmosphere of the conference (Faucher-King, 2005: 59). These expectations were partially satisfied: the party seemed renewed, rejuvenated, and democratic; and the New Labour leadership was defeated for the first time at conference only in 2000.[11]

The New Labour leaders tried to use individual members as a source of legitimation to demonstrate that the government enjoyed the support of the membership (ibid.: chapter 5). The establishment of direct relations between members and leaders—that is, bypassing the traditional intermediate elites—was presented as a guarantee of genuine consultation. However, the individualization of party relations was above all conceived as a way of creating a base that was simultaneously "massive" and "passive"—that is, supportive of leadership initiatives when called upon. Disappointing levels of participation were therefore scarcely a cause for surprise: internal elections regularly involved only a small fraction of members, in fact favoring the left of the party.[12] When participation was greater (as in the internal 1996 referendum on the election manifesto), the parliamentary leadership secured more clear-cut support, but at the cost of a very expensive internal campaign. In these conditions the party leadership preferred to keep the old rules (giving greater weight to the unions), particularly for the election of the national leader, and the Welsh and Scottish leaders, and for the selection of candidates, which make it possible to influence the results thanks to union support.

The intense recruitment campaign conducted with a view to the 1997 general election enabled the party to achieve 400,000 individual members. However, ten years later, the number was down below 200,000. How is this rapid reversal to be explained? Ten years in government had extinguished enthusiasm and dreams of change. Moreover, it proved difficult to secure the loyalty of new members (significant turnover of members), to mobilize them during operations to legitimate decisions via internal referendums (disappointing turnout), or even to influence them (during elections for party posts). Thus, the professed project of building a campaigning party with a mass membership, but isolated and docile, was not really accomplished (Farrell and Webb, 2000). Instead, New Labour devalued the notion of membership and significant participation, by fueling a culture of distrust of politicians and through the creation of new supporters' networks (Gauja, 2009).

A "Managed" and Disciplined Party

The organizational changes introduced by the New Labour team were not imposed on a reluctant party by an innovative, radical leadership, but the result of extended negotiated processes (Russell, 2005), some of which derived from the left of the party and were then instrumentalized by the modernizers. Rule changes (organizational reform of delegate selection, procedures for discussion, elections, and decisions) were insufficient to revolutionize the party. The New Labour team was also determined to transform the internal culture—in particular, the codes governing interaction between activists, and ways of expressing and conducting oneself in public. The institutionalization of New Labour was effected by eradicating traces of workerism and demonstrating the party's professionalization. The annual conference, display case of the organization par excellence,[13] was obviously central in this strategy; it provided an opportunity to influence perceptions of the right way to behave as a "good" Labour man or woman. During the 1970s and 1980s, the Labour Party conference had resembled a prize fight: party factions took the opportunity to clash publicly and measure their influence; leaders were frequently laid into. The policy debate may have been rich, but the general impression was of a cacophony and anarchy not conducive to persuading voters that Labour offered a credible alternative to the Conservative government.

Between 1994 and 2001, the year when they realized that they could not completely dissociate themselves from their old activists, the modernizers sought to alter the way of "being Labour." "Colleague" replaced "comrade"; violet and multicolor mosaics were substituted for the red background of official speeches and press conferences; and the hymn "The Red Flag" disappeared in favor of pop songs. The delegates who spoke from the podium were carefully selected and encouraged to be positive. They received advice on dress and could practice the text of their speech in front of specialists in the dramatic arts. Activists were called upon to defend the party and not provide opponents with arguments against it. They were warned against the presence of the press during the party's semipublic meetings (policy forums, national and local conferences). During conference, the New Labour leadership sought to persuade members that they were in a panopticon, constantly being observed and judged: the slightest disagreement could be interpreted by the press as evidence of a party that was divided and hence incapable of governing. A quasi-paranoia was fostered, and its effect was twofold. The atmosphere of these meetings was transformed: the sometimes bellicose chaos and intense policy debates gave way to smooth stage-managing. Speakers sang the praises of the government. They also referred to their personal experience, because everyone had understood the message of the communications advisors: to get a message across, you have to invoke the human dimension and stress the individual, "authentic" character of experience. In addition, participants disciplined themselves out of a fear of harming their party's prospects. Even the left wing, which was very hostile, was largely domesticated initially.

Change therefore also took the form of a voluntary erosion of the old, sometimes outdated processes that helped to foster the party's imagination and nostalgia. This "modernization" was certainly fought by the left, but it also affected long-standing activists by depriving them of the symbols and rites that contributed to their identification with the party. In this sense, the strategy of the team around Blair met with undoubted success: it transformed the image of Labour in public opinion and in the party. An unexpected consequence was the acceleration in the spiral of demobilization that has struck all British parties in the last two decades.

When the influx of new members dried up after the electoral victory of 1997, it was difficult to preserve the loyalty of isolated members. All levels of the party were called on to open meetings up to the least involved members, to abolish the organization committees of local groups, and to select as conference delegates members who had never participated in it before. The New Labour elites presented this development as a sign of democratization (the party now escaping from the control of activists and unions). The consequences for modes of political commitment, as well as their motivation, were more significant than anticipated: like their Conservative opponents, Labour benefited from the voluntary work of members, one of whose satisfactions was belonging to the movement. However, treated like consumers, they proved less and less loyal or devoted to an organization with which they no longer really identified (Seyd and Whiteley, 1992). But the party had neither the means to offer sufficient material remuneration to its activists (in the form of positions in local councils or the internal structure), nor the resources completely to replace the work of volunteers by that of employees. In this sense, renunciation of a strong working-class Labour identity, and the partial rejection of the collective past, helped transform the party. From 2001 the party readopted a few of its old symbols and some—including Gordon Brown—ostensibly abandoned the prefix, presenting themselves as "Labour."

A Search for Effective and Professional Funding

The change in internal culture was visible in other dimensions of the party's activity, such as control of the party's image (name, logo, events), or the professionalization of its funding. Until the 1990s the trade unions were the main contributors to the party (96 percent of the party's income in 1983), and also took responsibility for funding campaigns and some candidates. The New Labour elites strove to lessen this dependency by increasing the share of individual contributions and diversifying sources of income. From 1997 the unions contributed no more than 40 percent of the party's annual budget,[14] a proportion equal to that of small private contributions. Financial independence from the unions was made possible by the professionalization and subcontracting of fund-raising activities (Webb, 2000). New sources of finance were found, from individual sympathizers kept on board by automatic debits or generous contributors, whether anonymous (particularly in the case of loans) or not.

Today, on the American model, British election campaigns are quasi-permanent, and the professionalization of party communications involves considerable expenditure.[15] Parties subcontract functions previously performed by their activists and employees, such as the administration of membership files or the organization of conferences. New Labour no longer makes do with mobilizing its activists to carry out door-to-door canvassing, but uses the services of private firms for a number of campaign activities (particularly telephone canvassing and the organization of media events).[16]

Productivity improved, but professionalization entailed an increase in the party's funding requirements. New Labour therefore embarked upon commercial activities. From 1996 they learned from Henry Drucker, former head of fund-raising at Oxford University, why the Conservatives increasingly appealed to wealthy individuals whose contributions did not have to be declared. Parties had to find ways of circumventing legislation on the declaration of gifts to satisfy the concerns of potential donors. They studied the strategies developed in the United States, especially the possibility of offering or selling access to ministers, even to the prime minister. New Labour emulated this example and secured larger individual contributions.[17]

Elected on a pledge to clean up public life, in 2000 Labour adopted legislation requiring the declaration of private gifts and regulating the contributions of private individuals and corporate bodies. However, the commercial activities of parties, now rapidly expanding, eluded strict controls. In subsequent years, the Conservatives and New Labour diversified their funding thanks to the organization of receptions and charity dinners, the transformation of their annual conference into a fair-exhibition, or the "sale of services" (for example, private meetings with members of the government).[18] The discovery of such possibilities of legal funding, and the enthusiasm displayed by the party leadership for such an entrepreneurial strategy, was a clear break with the practices of prudent management inherited from the working-class tradition and distrust of the world of business (Drucker, 1979).

This organizational revolution coincided with a resolutely pluralistic and competitive approach to the political, to beat the Conservatives using the same financial weapons. The New Labour elites had no fears about advertising their penchant for wealthy entrepreneurs or their growing financial dependence on them.[19] Such practices were the cause of a police investigation into corruption. With the approach of the 2005 general election, New Labour, like the Conservatives, resorted to private loans that were exempt from public declaration under legislation on the financing of political life. Some of these loans (the sum total of which exceeded £23 million) were due for repayment in 2007, placing the party on the verge of a financial crisis.[20] The interest rates involved, which were very significantly below market rates, and the absence of any repayment date, potentially made them secret gifts. Ultimately, several ministers (including Tony Blair himself—the first time such a thing had happened) were questioned in the context of a police enquiry into the ennoblement of several benefactors.[21] This inquiry intensified the discrediting of the prime minister and New Labour, who had presented themselves in 1997 as ethical entrepreneurs and incorruptible.[22]

The Party as Communications Enterprise

Moreover, the party's organization was profoundly revised in a direction that anticipated the reforms implemented by the government from 1997 onward. Appointed general-secretary of the party in 1994, Tom Sawyer came from a trade union background and the left of the party. Less than ten weeks after he had taken up his post, he presented a plan for reorganizing the party's National Executive Committee. Some months later, he organized training workshops at the Cranfield School of Management. Convinced of the need to change rules and practices alike, he wanted to make the party a more efficient organization, one that was highly reactive and creative. He hoped that introducing "new management" into the party would also make it possible to enhance its ability to anticipate the attacks of political opponents, be it the Conservative Party (and, to a lesser extent, the Liberal Democrats) or the media. Sawyer wanted to change mind-sets and alter working methods. Following the Conservatives, New Labour gradually adopted the model of the firm.[23]

The party therefore gradually developed new tools for forecasting and supervision, quality control, and new ways of motivating and assessing employees and activists. From 1995 onward, all levels of the party had to present action plans, establish priorities, indicate objectives, and then audit their practices and results. New performance indicators imposed holding policy forums and the opening up of meetings of local executives to members. Occasional working groups were created to solve urgent problems, and teams were dispatched to reorganize local sections that were in difficulty. Models of good practice were disseminated. The party's fundamental objectives (and not just clause 4) were revisited in order to reflect on better means of internal communication.

The working atmosphere at headquarters was profoundly changed by the party's move from John Smith House (in south London) to Westminster. At the outset, only the campaign team was installed in Millbank. But it was followed in 1998 by all departments, which were reorganized in new interior-designed offices. Furthermore, the party began to outsource services, particularly those for members, in order to take advantage of the less onerous cost of living outside London. It called more systematically on subcontractors, external advisors, and public relations professionals. This trend accelerated after the 1997 victory, when the volunteers and temporary staff involved in the campaign returned to their normal occupations but continued to work for the party on an occasional free-lance basis.

Discussion and Control of the Policy Agenda

The Labour Party used to be a polycephalous organization characterized by a multiplicity of sites of policy discussion and decision-making. Neil Kinnock had already sought to strengthen the leadership's influence over policy directions. At the end of the 1980s, the policy review process had made it possible to abandon those proposals that were most radical and unpopular with the electorate (especially unilateral nuclear disarmament) (Shaw, 1993). But the party constitution asserted the sovereignty of the annual party conference and its central role in formulating policy.

Two complementary analyses and a constraint inspired the reform of the procedures for adopting policy. First, the conference must be able to retain a key role in the system, if only to adopt and legitimate decisions.[24] Secondly, it had to be capable of being used as a showcase for the unity, the dynamism, and the professionalism of a party that had been modernized and liberated from its old demons. Finally, since the success of a future Labour government depended on its ability to retain the support of its base, a two-way system of communication had to be ensured, making it possible not only to relay social demands upward but also to facilitate the legitimation of government policies, their explanation and promotion on the public agenda.

Reflection on the processes of policy-formation was initiated at the end of the 1980s, fed by experiments conducted in the party's social movements and women's sections. Initially, it focused on increasing individual participation, promoting members, and widening the representation of minorities. The Swedish Social Democratic Party was taken as a significant example of effective collaboration between leadership and activist rank-and-file. When Tony Blair was elected leader, a majority of Labour Party members believed that existing discussion procedures produced redundant, even contradictory and incoherent texts. In addition, these procedures were dominated by organized factions, the trade unions, and the leadership. The emergence of a consensus on the malfunctioning of conference procedures made possible the introduction of institutions that were presented as more open, effective, and democratic. It was in the name of membership participation that the Labour Party altered its internal modus operandi.

At the same time, the party's moderate left became aware of the negative impact of the public character of debates on the image of the party and the quality of discussions. This made it possible to justify shifting decision-making sites and exercising constant control over conduct and communications activities. Having emerged in the course of a process of practical experimentation from 1986 onward, policy forums were a way of consulting the activists at the base and inviting outside experts and representatives of different interest groups. The reform's promoters were convinced that the new process would necessarily lead to a consensus on the "right" solutions, discussed and amended in private before appearing on the stage of public debate.

The 1997 program "Partnership in Power" institutionalized a process of ongoing thematic reflection, by creating a national policy forum that comprised representatives of the membership, the unions, and the party leadership (all of them elected for two years) under the auspices of the government. The major policy axes (economy, health, education, and so forth) were regularly reworked over two-year periods. Thus, a new policy draft was written by a special committee and discussed in local and national forums. The intermediate report and the final product were amended by the national forum and submitted to the annual conference for approval. In theory, the government's pivotal role in the committees ensured close collaboration between leaders and activists. No provision had been made for a mechanism that guaranteed the expression of divergent viewpoints and effective communication upward. In the past the party's legalistic tradition had made it possible to force negotiations on the leaders. But the new rules were less explicit and indirectly favored an increase in the role of the executive.

From 1998 the forums were used as tools for legitimating policies adopted by the government. If the members, and their representatives in the national policy forum, were invited to contribute to debates (including by the use of electronic means of communication), the methods adopted to take account of these contributions remained underdeveloped. Procedures that were supposed to facilitate the emergence of a consensus predominantly served to promote government policies. Far from decentralizing discussions, New Labour concentrated power in order constantly to project the image of a united party to the outside world. This controlling practice was also inspired by the conviction that the government possessed the information and resources required to guide the discussions toward the optimal political solutions. Thus, any disagreement was seen as requiring further pedagogical efforts by the leaders. The private sessions did not escape this search for cohesion, and the private expression of disagreements was checked because the government remained largely deaf to suggestions from Labour's ranks.

The reform had been conceived to prevent the appearance of a rift between the government and its base. It was a qualified success. Whereas previous Labour governments had never been able to stay in power for two full successive terms, Tony Blair's party won three massive election victories. Such results were not obtained against the activists or the party. Nevertheless, once the honeymoon of the first government was over, and the anguish of an election defeat in 2001 avoided, the divergences became more marked, particularly over the funding of public services. The government then presented itself as the guarantor of the interests of citizen-consumers against the opinion of self-selected activists. As a result, many activists had the feeling that the forums had been introduced to neutralize them, rather than to listen to them (Faucher-King, 2005: 184). Now without a sense of being able to contribute to the political life of their party, some left it. Others reduced their investment, so that many internal positions are now held by political entrepreneurs, often employed by the trade unions or MPs, think tanks, local government, the press, or consultancy and lobbying firms (Dunleavy, 2006: 333). The guiding line of the reforms faded and the party was subjected to a reformist activism that aimed to establish flexibility, but which primarily led to links being dissolved and founding democratic principles being brought into question.

New Labour's Media Offensive

In 1986 Neil Kinnock created the Shadow Communications Agency (SCA), in order to improve the party's reception among the upwardly mobile classes and promote an image of competence and professionalism. Additional efforts were made thereafter to ensure that the party's image was not only positive but also fine-tuned. When the modernizing team led by Tony Blair assumed the leadership of the Labour Party in 1994, one of its first concerns was to take charge of the tools of communication. The slogan "New Labour, New Britain" made its appearance during Tony Blair's first national conference. In subsequent years, without ever having been debated and approved by a party body, the neologism was repeated like a mantra until it became established as self-evident. In fact, the party changed its name without undergoing the trauma of being refounded. Party communications were also centralized from 1996: the rose of the logo, stylized, was registered as a trademark and then imposed on all local groups. This offensive aimed at charming and reassuring the Conservative press. A more hands-on approach to relations with the media ensured a coherent message and made it possible to influence interpretations of the news offered by journalists. Spin was complemented by the establishment of a line of communication to candidates and MPs in 1996.

Such a change of attitude involved recourse to discipline both within the parliamentary cohort and among activists. Initially, control over every detail of the party's external communications was justified by the desire to win power in a very hostile media environment.[25] Moreover, Labour's base responded positively to a strategy that conformed to the determination to win elections.

The Labour Party's communications revolution was made possible because the communications advisors, particularly Alastair Campbell[26] and Peter Mandelson, had prior professional experience of the media. Without hesitation, they used their intimate knowledge of the pressures, rivalries, and motivations of the journalistic milieu for the party's benefit. New Labour thus refined selective leaking and exclusive or progressive announcements. They standardized all their communications and supplied ready-made interpretations. In this way, they maximized their impact on the media agenda. Their approach was radically innovatory, because it reversed priorities: henceforth "communication was not something that you tagged on the end, it is part of what you do,"[27] because the interpretation of public policy and political actions was indissociable from the reputation of the party brand. Use of the services of communications professionals enabled the party to exercise tighter control over the way in which political information was presented.

In the space of a few years, the party constructed an effective strategy and team, securing the cooperation of some of the media and manipulating the rest.[28] The formidable communications machine honed by New Labour in opposition also served to organize the relations between the new government and the media. Government spending on publicity grew dramatically, reaching £203 million in 2004–5. In the same period the government employed seventy-two communications advisors. Trapped in a relationship of dependency as regards information, which was released strategically and parsimoniously by official sources, some of the media denounced the triumph of propaganda over substance. These tensions resulted not only in a rebellion by various reputable political journalists, who were frustrated at no longer being able to obtain exclusives, but also in increasing attention being paid to the political processing, the "fabrication" of information, and the production of government statistics. Having achieved mastery in the manipulation of information and rebuttal,[29] the Labour Party engaged in a permanent electoral campaign that justified the work of experts all year round.

Over the last decade, the British media landscape has become more complex and segmented as a result of the expansion of electronic technologies, the deregulation of the telecommunications market, and the concentration of firms. Although competition on the air has existed since 1955 (the creation of ITV), the major change dates from the introduction of cable and satellite and the creation of the Sky Television (BSkyB) package in 1989. Aside from the multiplication of channels, the most important innovation has unquestionably been the creation of new channels that broadcast continuously and the development of fierce competition in both the audiovisual sector and the written press. One can debate the "tabloidization" of the media and the increasing marginalization of political news. But the diversification and segmentation of sources of information are striking, as is the personalization of politics and recourse to slogans. Thus, while political parties can theoretically target their communications and address new, clearly defined audiences, they are also less capable of controlling the message that is broadcast. Politics has been banalized in the mass media, which resorts to a theatrical presentation of male and female politicians in order to entertain the public.

Unable to allow themselves to be caught out by their political opponents, Labour (and the Conservatives) now concentrate on consensual themes and strive for total control over the form of their representation in the media. To a great extent this transformation has been facilitated in the United Kingdom by the expansion of the public relations industry to a degree that is unknown in most Continental European countries (Faucher-King, 2005: chapter 6; Miller and Dinan, 2000). This new economic sector emerged from 1979 and developed thanks to the privatization and deregulation campaigns initiated by Thatcher. During the 1990s these firms asserted their influence because the government itself and political parties began to be concerned with their image and presentation. As a result, it became ever more difficult to distinguish information from activities of self-promotion and news management developed by highly professionalized political parties. Parties strove to combine favorable presentation of their "product" and recourse to particular interpretations of events. In a sense, passive adaptation to an anticipated future helped create its own reality. The perfecting of techniques of media manipulation during the phase of winning power, and subsequent employment of the same techniques to communicate the Labour government's initiatives, encouraged a latent cynicism that reached a peak during the second Blair government.

Spin had damaging effects on the relations between political parties and the press and fueled growing disillusionment with the media on the part of the British electorate, creating an unprecedented crisis of confidence in political parties. Various slip-ups helped to expose the excesses of this news manipulation and exacerbated public skepticism. One of the most famous examples is a memorandum written by the transport secretary's press officer: concerned about the results of independent inquiries into fatal accidents on the railways, following the 11 September attacks on New York it announced that now was "a good day to bury bad news."

Political journalists gradually learned to clear away a proliferation of redundant statements intended to create a media splash. While such practices made it possible to highlight government efforts for a time, in the medium term they generated cynicism in journalists and the public. Thus, the New Labour government was frequently accused of making illusion prevail over substance, of privileging the image over the reality of policy decisions.[30]

Blair's language and New Labour's rhetoric were remarkable engines for success, but with time they came under severe criticism. The end of the prime minister's mandate was especially difficult for this reason. Tony Blair's language was characterized, in particular, by binary formulas that affected to reconcile opposites—for example, "traditional values in a modern setting." The communications strategy exploited the leader's skills and personalized Labour's image. Blair presented himself as an ordinary man, a family man, candid and direct, who did not encumber himself with complicated grand formulas. He played on British pragmatism, even anti-intellectualism. But having long pointed to his sincerity, it became more difficult for him to maintain his credibility following engagement in the Iraq war alongside the Americans. In fact, the press revealed how the skillful presentation of dossiers from the intelligence agencies succeeded in fooling Parliament and how the government resorted to calumny to discredit hostile intelligence sources, leading to the suicide of one of the experts involved. The revelation that the government had committed itself even before it had secured UN support fueled resentment. From 2003, conscious of the saturation of information and the harmful effects of attempts to control news, New Labour unavailingly sought to prove that it had abandoned its endeavor to control the media agenda completely.

Changes in the mediatization of British political life are doubtless inevitable in the age of the triumph of reality TV programs. Confronted with the competition of more amusing news, political parties seek to offer the media (in particular, the audiovisual media) photogenic and telegenic elements, stories that are prepackaged and also increasingly "human." From the standpoint of election campaigns, the comings and goings of personalities—especially Labour ministers—are meticulously prepared, in order to ensure that the local media can witness "spontaneous" encounters with an enthusiastic crowd (composed not of citizens who happen to be present, but of specially mobilized activists, or even actors). Parties have ceased to be forums of public debate and focus their efforts on presenting individual, moving experiences that justify their political projects and promoting personalities.

In their efforts to improve their chances of electoral victory, parties of government try to win over the average voter. To do this, they adapt their product to the supposed expectations of their consumers and present themselves as teams of competent managers. They concentrate on consensual themes (Farrell and Webb, 2002). However, the competition is losing much of its interest and politics no longer involves resolving conflicts and societal choices. The flourishing of a managerial model of governance has helped reinforce the image of elected representatives as remote from citizens' concerns.

During the 1990s, parties sought to present themselves as "listening" and increasingly resorted to the services of professionals in communications and political marketing, charged with exploring the demands of the average citizen and helping parties to appear responsive to those demands. Such developments do not require the contribution of the traditional activist working on the ground with voters, or in policy reflection and formation. The demobilization of the British public and growing electoral apathy are bound up with the imposition of a seeming consensus and overly rigid control of the terms of the debate. The New Labour governments relied on the party while transforming it profoundly, seeking to domesticate it once and for all and undermining the role of parties in general in British political life. The hemorrhage of activists that it has suffered in the last ten years is often attributed to Tony Blair's unpopularity and the war in Iraq. But the destabilization might be more profound, for political structures and cultures have been altered. The Conservatives hope to profit from this, but the credibility of all political parties emerges weakened from the New Labour experience.

5   Democratization or Control?

The reforms I have set out will transform our politics. They will re-draw the boundaries between what is done in the name of the people and what is done by the people themselves. They will create a new relationship between government and the people, based on trust, freedom, choice and responsibility. . . . [T]hey are deeply political reforms because they are concerned with the essence of our democracy and how people can exercise power in our society.
    —Tony Blair, *New Britain: My Vision for a Young Country*, 1996

Historically, British democracy has privileged individuals and their rights. The transformation of democracy, and opening up of opportunities for all individuals regardless of their origin, turned out to be at the heart of New Labour policy, whether that involved depoliticizing certain elements of the decision-making process or mobilizing individuals and local communities in an original way. The activist state of the Blair governments privileged individuals (as consumers and local or religious communities) and small groups. Blairite British democracy took the form of a multiplication of experiments in citizens' participation in public administration, of an injunction to participate: "Organize and participate, be autonomous, and the state will help you by strictly defining the rules of the game." The promise of a Britain open to the world and at ease with itself, implicit in the slogan "Cool Britannia," had been strengthened by hopes of a lasting peace in Northern Ireland. But the invasion of Iraq, and new terrorist threats (which materialized when four young Muslims blew themselves up with their bombs in the London underground and buses on 7 July 2005, killing fifty-two people and wounding several dozens), soon clouded the picture. New Labour "democratization" resulted in an individualization of relations to the political and the mobilization of small groups; it combined an internalization of constraint and increasing ability to participate for some with greater exercise of government control.

The Citizen-Consumer

The image of the citizen as consumer of public services emerged during the Thatcher years alongside two other types of actor: the taxpayer, who seeks to maximize the efficiency of his or her taxes; and the "scrounger," who lives off various benefits. Consumers of public services are honest users, but in search of quality and a match between their needs and the services provided (Clarke, 2004). The Citizens' Charters introduced by the Conservatives aimed to create distance between the government and the services and to present the government as the defender of the public against the interests of providers. This approach was adopted by New Labour from 1999 and generalized: citizens were encouraged to use their purchasing power to influence the decisions of markets and service providers.

The modernization of public administration led to collective approaches being challenged in favor of individual approaches. The New Labour government promoted the idea of a personalization of services, which implied consumers' involvement in deciding the quality and character of the service sought (education, social aid, or medical care). The logic of personalization downgraded demands from the unions that defended service providers.

The figure of the consumer is now dominant in public policy; it has gradually replaced that of the patient, the pupil, or the passenger. This strategy is manifestly not taken at face value by British people. Only a fraction (20 percent) of those using services (for example, health care or the police) identify themselves as consumers.[1] The idea of choice is likewise greeted with ambivalence, because what exists above all is a desire for improved services in terms of expertise, trust, and convenience of use. Although choice is presented as "what people want," the public continues to prioritize the quality of services (ibid.).

The weakness of the concept of citizenship in the British context no doubt explains why New Labour sought to associate with it less contested concepts, like the individual, the consumer, and the community, in order to foreground both the rights and the duties of individuals.[2] The rhetoric employed by the government interchangeably used the phrases "the citizen as consumer," "the citizen or the consumer," and "the citizen-consumer." It became a leitmotif of draft policies and synonymous with liberalization and democratization, because consumer choices were construed as inherently liberating inasmuch as they confer power on individuals. Two different registers were mixed in these linguistic games. The first—that of citizenship—invokes collective action and intervention in public life, as well as the existence of collective identities, particularly national identity. The second pertains to the register of the individual and the private, market exchange guided by a logic of choice, calculations, and preferences, and detached from any reference to a collective identity. Thinking in terms of consumers foregrounds the market relationship between individuals and contrasts with the figure of the citizen, an actor bound up with a collective of rights and relations of solidarity. Political practice has undoubtedly been transformed by a quarter-century of reforms placing *homo economicus*— the egoistic, rational, calculating individual—at the heart of government thinking about economics and politics.

Where, in the past, politics in the United Kingdom was analyzed in accordance with its collectivist currents,[3] the contemporary landscape is quite different. Collective identities that long structured party competition and favored a strong social alignment of the vote have been largely eroded. John Major, and then Tony Blair after him, claimed that they wanted to create a classless society, and to increase opportunities for upward social mobility and success for the most deserving. These projects took concrete shape in public policy encouraging the individualization of relations to the political and lauding the merits of the pursuit of individual self-interest. Moreover, many political problems were now presented as technical problems requiring personalized solutions. As in other democracies, collective forms of engagement (trade unions and parties) are in decline, and the proportion of British people who believe that "citizens have a moral duty to engage in local political life" has fallen from 70 percent in 1959 (Almond and Verba, 1963) to 44 percent in 2000 (Pattie et al., 2004: 272). In 1959, 6 percent of those questioned declared themselves in favor of passivity; in 2000 the figure was 18 percent. Attitudes have changed as regards the areas in which government is supposed to intervene and where citizens can make an impact.

An "Individualized" Activism?

Work done in the context of a citizenship audit suggests that there is neither a decline in interest in politics (in the broad sense), nor a reduction in engagement. What has changed are the modes of political engagement: over a period of twelve months, three out of four people perform at least one type of action aimed at influencing rules, laws, and public policy. However, a majority of those acts involve little or any contact with others. The most popular activities consist of financial donations (two-thirds of respondents), fund-raising for an organization (one-third of respondents), and signature of a petition (half of respondents). Furthermore, the political consumerism adopted by New Labour has become part of normal behavior: 41 percent of British people have boycotted a product and 39 percent have bought something for political reasons.[4] Individualized forms of participation (Micheletti, 2003), and especially monetary forms of mobilization, contrast with the collectivist period when membership in a trade union was the norm and engagement was based on a strong sense of collective action and solidarity. The industrial crisis and the Thatcher governments have destroyed that working-class, male model.

Tony Blair frequently used the language of enlightened individualism as a justification for his policy proposals.[5] This approach, which he regarded as democratic and nonideological, is based on challenging traditional forms of political action and on faith in an "invisible hand" regulating economic and political conflicts.[6] For New Labour the egoism of the citizen-consumer engaging in decisions that concern him personally makes it possible to encourage individuals to take responsibility, and to exercise their freedom as consumers by intervening on the supply-side or mobilizing in a community framework.

What was most specific about the New Labour governmental experience was that it relied on the enlistment and mobilization of citizens and local communities, of associations. Organizations assessing and participating in the management of facilities or programs multiplied and encouraged participation. The parents of pupils, users of services, but also groups neglected or scorned by the Conservatives (women, ethnic minorities,[7] the disabled, the sick, and so forth) were welcomed en masse. All those with a stake in public services were called upon to express their preferences and participate. This was the "democratization" plank of modernization, whose importance was decisive: civil society penetrated public organizations, institutions, and public services. Interest groups or minorities thus found themselves appointed to decision-making and assessment roles at all levels of the public services, from the local municipal library to the national commission dealing with the introduction of a minimum wage. Participation was nevertheless subject to a significant constraint: obeying indicators. The government retained two major prerogatives: control over indicators and financial penalties.

Social Entrepreneurs and Local Communities

The citizen-consumer is now active in a participation market in which they can take advantage of increased opportunities. In order to encourage local initiative and self-organization by groups, the government granted autonomy and budgets to associations charged with personalizing, for example, the public services of education or health. New Labour wanted to extend the opportunities offered to individuals, but those rights were combined with a requirement for individual responsibility (or family responsibility, given that parents get involved in schools in order to ensure the best opportunities for their offspring). The beneficiaries of these openings were therefore "social entrepreneurs" and the middle classes. Studies of participation in formal or informal groups reveal that those who participate most have the highest incomes, are the best educated, and are the most favored socially. Studies of political engagement indicate that the least well off citizens in terms of income, status, and educational level are most frequently in favor of interventionist policies by the state (especially as regards social policy). But these fringes of society are also those least likely to participate in the political process or get involved in committees, because they feel excluded, illegitimate, incompetent, and impotent.

As a result, whereas direct participation by citizens and community associations was given priority, signaling a radical change in the administration of different social services or schools, references to solidarity or equality were rare or avoided altogether. The argument was as follows: uniformity is a source of inequalities (because the wealthy can choose to opt out of the system). Choice must be offered to the greatest number (in order to serve the individual needs of consumers better). In this sense, Tony Blair's governments essentially defended the interests of the middle and upper classes, who wanted access to better public services. By contrast, providing services to the rest was not a priority. This elitist vision made possible an improvement in the quality of services, limiting the development of a completely two-speed system. By laying so much stress on performance, the Blair governments hoped to enable the whole population to enjoy improved services.

The image of Labour as a party that referred to the working class, and the defense of all those who were excluded, had been analyzed as a major electoral handicap, which New Labour successfully strove to counter (Jowell et al., 1994). New Labour presented itself as the party of the aspiring middle classes, of social entrepreneurs, of "working families." The social categories that participate the least are also those whose interests have the least chance of being taken into consideration. What are the consequences of a system in which participation is socially structured to the detriment of the least advantaged, and in which public decisions tend to favor groups that can defend their interests? The widening of inequalities that began during the Thatcher years scarcely decreased under the Blair governments. On the other hand, attitudes toward the poor changed. Between 1994 and 2003 the percentage of those who thought that poverty was a question of social justice declined from 30 percent to 19 percent; in 2007, 28 percent of British people thought that the poor were shirkers—the figure had stood at only 15 percent in 1994 (Armstrong, 2003).

Virtual Engagement and Real Funding

Forms of engagement by British citizens have been transformed into individual forms that are often monetary.[8] According to *The Times*,[9] 700,000 individuals in 2002 engaged by donating more than £200 million over a period of five years by signing up for automatic payments. Charity organizations have long maintained a presence in Britain's high streets, but competition and professionalization encouraged an escalation in door-to-door canvassing:[10] individual canvassing makes it possible to test out the target audience and particularly to mobilize younger benefactors. The new technologies make it possible to target audiences with great precision; they then become the prey of constant mail.[11] These developments echo New Labour's modernizing ambitions for its own members and the tendency to promote forms of party membership that entail scarcely more effort than involvement in the venerable Royal Society for the Protection of Birds (RSPB). A dramatic increase in membership is a source of legitimacy and credibility (the RSPB had more than a million members in 1997, compared with 100,000 in 1972) in organizations that are sometimes controlled by far from democratic oligarchies.

But if donations might lead us to imagine a high degree of (financial) mobilization by British citizens, the new modes of participation above all reveal a strong tendency to delegate participation in public life to groups that are deemed more effective. Thus, cyber-activism often emerges as an alternative to activism in a local group. In fact, the relations developed by this new type of individualized mobilization are not horizontal—creating links with other activists in local groups—but vertical and imaginary.[12] What is involved are virtual communities of activists, frequently appealing to the Internet, that are imagined through recourse to symbols with a plurality of meanings and with the support of celebrities who have temporarily enrolled to promote a cause and stress its human dimension. "Debit card" participants in a sense subcontract their political involvement to bodies created and led by political entrepreneurs. In the United States this development favors groups for whom the issue of participation is not relevant, because they are content to mobilize supporters financially. They launch campaigns according to the prospects and constraints of political marketing by appealing to various professionals.[13] Initiatives are launched by leaders and conducted with well-targeted media campaigns, such as the "Make Poverty History" campaign in 2005, or those over environmental perils.

Far from seeking participation, the most visible groups now focus on media campaigns, lobbying, and expertise. Participation is not deliberative, and public debate remains minimal. In fact, political debate is restricted to a dialogue between professional lobbyists, elected officials, and civil servants. A very important organization in Britain like the Ramblers (which brings together walkers and campaigns for the maintenance and upkeep of hiking paths) calls on the public to join as follows: "By becoming a member you are helping to ensure our work continues. In return we will provide you with a range of benefits to help you get the most out of walking."[14] The aim of large groups is not to offer their members a forum in which to discuss the policies to pursue. In exchange for their contribution, members can receive benefits (access to the RSPB's bird sanctuaries, hiking maps, and so forth) and preferential information on the lobbying activities conducted in their name. Traditional collectivist organizations seek to follow this example and, during the 1980s and 1990s, several trade unions tried to offer individual incentives that answered to the expectations of the new citizen-consumers.[15]

Checkbook activism has become one of the dominant modes of engagement, including for associations that originally had a vocation of local activity. Integration into policy networks allows large activist organizations (particularly multinational ones, like Greenpeace or Amnesty International) to offer their members an apparent guarantee of effectiveness. In addition, the expansion of the voluntary and charitable sector, and the considerable finance it generates, have led to the creation of audit agencies that claim to offer the generous actors of British public life ways of assessing and comparing the supply of charitable activity on the ultracompetitive market of good works. In case of dissatisfaction, it is always possible to find different organizations supplying comparable services and more appropriate selective incentives. This mode of political engagement contrasts with the new social movements that, in the 1970s and 1980s, demanded a deepening of representative democracy.

Not-for-profit organizations are presented as important factors in democracy in the United Kingdom not because they are themselves democratic, but because they contribute to an image of pluralism and personalized participation tailored to individual demand. Encouraged by Conservative governments and then Labour ones, the third sector has grown significantly in terms of the number of paid jobs and hours of voluntary work in social, cultural, sporting, or health sectors.[16] On account of this growth, a number of organizations are involved in commercial activities or have entered into contractual relations with the state, so as to reduce their dependence on members and less regular contributors. For these organizations, patronage and expertise offer routes to access and influence that are much more rapid and effective than mobilizing members. They help to facilitate access to the status of co-optee into policy networks linked to Whitehall. In effect, nongovernmental organizations play a role in the formation of public policy as well as its delivery. Quasi Nongovernmental Organizations (Quangos) and agencies have helped to involve individuals in public policy networks without necessarily ensuring openness and transparency. They have been dominated by pressure groups, and the impact of consolidating received ideas in small groups has sometimes been disastrous, especially in the area of agriculture and food.[17]

Particular interest groups (and also local communities) are proliferating. They seek to obtain benefits for their target group while limiting the costs to themselves and thus expanding the base of contributors. Faced with these contradictory demands, the state is tempted to play a supervisory, regulatory role and leave individual and collective social actors to adjust to the rules of the game. New Labour formed part of this scenario. For it, democratization essentially consisted in opening up new individual opportunities and guaranteeing the exercise of certain rights. Emulating other left-wing governments in Europe, New Labour adopted important laws on recognizing the rights of homosexuals (lowering the legal age of consent for homosexual relationships to that for heterosexuals),[18] against marital violence, and for children's rights. They also engaged vigorously with sexual equality and in opposition to discrimination against ethnic minorities. Not only was the Commission on Racial Equality strengthened but efforts were also made to identify and combat institutional racism. Racist attacks and insults are now crimes. The police and the army were encouraged to promote officers originating in the Caribbean or the Indian subcontinent. Despite criticisms from an extraordinarily hostile press, conditions for the reception and detention of immigrants and asylum-seekers were improved.

Finally, the European Convention on Human Rights was ratified. This record marked considerable progress for Britain after the Conservative years and the xenophobic excesses of that party's right wing. Moreover, the country acted as a magnet attracting immigrants to Europe, largely as a result of the liberalization promoted by the Blair governments.

The multiplication of Quangos and agencies has also contributed to the depolitization of public decisions and management (Burnham, 2001), because "technical" problems are supposed to be most efficiently solved by experts. Thus the government can protect itself from the consequences of unpopular decisions while governing at arm's length. The responsibility for social change rests with individuals or with the agencies against which ordinary citizens have little influence (Freedland, 2001), but the government cannot be blamed when social demands are short term or sectoral.

Participatory Democracy, Democratic Illusion

The democratization of the British system also took the form of a challenge to social hierarchies, by introducing new rights to information, a direct and informal style of relationship with citizens, and experiments with new modes of governance and devolution. The atrophy of parties, and of certain organizations like trade unions, makes communication between citizens and political elites difficult. These organizations served, in effect, as intermediaries between citizens and the state ("facilitator" of exchanges in the economic and political market). The "era of pure representative democracy is drawing to a close," wrote Peter Mandelson in 1998, because "people want to be more directly involved." The solution lay in "plebiscites, focus groups, lobbies, 'citizens movements,' and the Internet" (Mandelson, cited in Paul Routledge, 1999: 277–78). The new technologies and the Internet were soon being presented as tools of modern democratic communication. The publication of reports and audits made it possible to ensure government transparency, but interactivity was also used as a way of bypassing intermediate groups. Labour MPs did not always maintain the desired discipline: they often preferred to bow to the demands of their direct electorate, rather than follow the voting instructions issued by the party (Cowley, 2005). The government sought to address voters directly, doubtless in the belief that, liberated from the influence of social groups, individuals would understand that their personal interest was best served by a government enlightened by experts. Taking control over relations with the press made it possible to develop top-down communication,[19] conceived as an education in government action. Communication from the bottom up was ensured by new consultative procedures justified in the name of deliberative democracy.[20] The party and the government multiplied blogs or question-and-answer sessions with ministers before launching in an Internet channel on Youtube in 2007.[21] But if the Internet promotes the circulation of information, it also conduces to a segmentation in relations to the political: there currently exist more than three thousand government sites (with the suffix .gov.uk), but less than 12 percent of citizens have had on-line dealings with the government;[22] 70 percent of British people were on-line in 2004, but only 17 percent used the Internet to find political information (Lusoli et al., 2006: 24–42).

The government also pursued at a national level the experiment with forums conducted in the party. From 1998 consultative groups were organized on the public services. The first, at the University of Birmingham, brought together five thousand people chosen by lottery and representative of the population; the experiment was extended to Scotland and regularly used at a local level. Various agencies also followed the example by organizing citizens' juries consulted on GMOs, the state of the BBC, nano-technology, or services for the elderly. In many cases the organization of these forums were outsourced to professionals such as Opinion Leader Research, which in 2005 conducted the largest "listening study ever to take place in England" (Opinion Leader Research, 2006: 1) on behalf of the NHS.[23] New Labour sponsored a number of events that were presented as so many opportunities to get a better knowledge of public expectations. Foundations, think tanks, and universities participated in the creation of groups facilitating such events. While the British public has more than ever been "listened to," it is not clear how these new processes indeed "empower" the public and open up political discussions. On the contrary, research indicates that they "restrict the range of topics and scope of solutions up for debate even while they increase the scale and depth of public input" (Lee, 2008: 28).[24]

However, public policy does not seem always to have taken into account the opinions expressed by citizens when questioned in this way. Juries on genetically modified organisms recommended a halt to commercialization and studies of their environmental impact, prior to the resumption of open-field tests. But the government adopted positions that were more open to scientific research and the commercialization of certain species (particularly corn).[25] The contrast between the government's rhetoric of deliberative democracy and the lack of influence of deliberative procedures on decisions was criticized on several occasions. After 1998 the Audit Commission emphasized both the difficulty involved in translating decisions imposed from on high into new participatory practices, and the inadequacies of forums and juries. In some cases the consultations were clearly dominated by the best-financed interest groups, at the expense of the quality of public debate. The government was itself condemned in 2007, following a complaint from Greenpeace about a consultative forum on renewing the nuclear energy stock, for having deliberately supplied incomplete and partial information to the participants: Tony Blair hastened to confirm that his government's policy would nevertheless not be changing.

Finally, in 2004 the government launched a "big conversation" by inviting the public to submit comments and suggestions on the issues of its choice by Internet or e-mail, text-message, letter, or telephone. The procedure was repeated in 2006. This operation formed part of continuing efforts by British political parties since the 1980s to seem as if they were "listening" to voters; it forms a perfect illustration of the process of individualization of relations to the political encouraged by New Labour. How could anyone think that a juxtaposition of monologues and text-messages, which received a stock letter by way of response, constitutes an effective consultation process capable of influencing government policies? The hypothesis is all the more unrealistic in that New Labour was already convinced in advance that it had arrived at pragmatic answers to social demands. Up to what point can processes for legitimating policy decisions prolong the illusion of democracy without undermining trust in political institutions? How lasting are the positive feelings experienced by those who have personally taken part in a forum or jury?

The Return of Protest

New Labour inadvertently encouraged the mobilization of many groups opposed to its policy, thus contributing to democratic debate in a rather different way. The citizenship audit revealed fluctuations in British potential for protest. High in the 1970s, very low after the lost battles with the Thatcher government, today it is experiencing a new lease on life (Pattie et al., 2004: 279). In 2001, 23 percent of British people were ready to demonstrate (Sanders et al., 2003; Pattie et al., 2003), while 81 percent believed that demonstrations were a legitimate way of making one's voice heard by government. In the absence of an effective parliamentary opposition since 1997, was political debate transferred from Parliament to the streets and the media?

In fact, large demonstrations became almost routine in British political life, mobilizing numerous intermediate groups. The record for turn-out had long been held by demonstrations against the Poll Tax,[26] which at the start of the 1990s attracted around 100,000 people and eventually cost Margaret Thatcher her job. During the Blair years, demonstrations were both more frequent and larger. They were no longer a preserve of the left: the right entered the arena, in particular with marches to defend rural life, against homosexuals, and against fuel taxes. A march by landowners alongside the Conservative leader was a sign of the routinization of such mobilizations. A peak was no doubt reached when ministers scrambled to participate in mobilizations provoked by the decisions of their own government! Thus, in 2006 the chair of the New Labour Party, Hazel Blears, took part in a march against the closure of a maternity hospital in her constituency. A few months earlier, Jacqui Smith, chief whip,[27] and Home Secretary John Reid were on the march. The latter justified his presence at a demonstration against the closure of accident and emergency services in his constituency by explaining that the gathering "is not organised. It's not the normal political or trade union demonstration. This is just ordinary people who know how much accident and emergency means to this area."[28]

Demonstrations by the Countryside Alliance in the streets of London mobilized 250,000 participants in 1998 and 400,000 in 2002; 200,000 marched against poverty in Scotland in 2005. The largest protest marches were prompted by the military intervention in Iraq: 400,000 demonstrated in October 2002 and then in March and April 2003. The march of 15 February 2003 brought together more than a million demonstrators.[29] On the eve of the 2006 Labour Party conference, 60,000 marched in the streets of Manchester against the occupation of Iraq and Afghanistan, budgetary constrictions in the health system, and to demand Blair's resignation. The tactics used now combined mobilization, lobbying, and media offensives.[30]

Did such passion signify that protest politics was effective? Not really. The New Labour governments in fact proved heedless of the protests; fox hunting was outlawed, Section 28[31] repealed, fuel taxes maintained. Finally, British troops were in Iraq from 2003 to 2009 and have remained in Afghanistan since 2001.

The frustration of the extraparliamentary left during the later Conservative governments had led some groups to resort to nonviolent direct action (Doherty et al., 2000). These new forms of mobilization had attacked road-building and airport development programs in particular. Installed in trees or underground tunnels, activists took significant physical risks to halt the works or alert public opinion. With the slowing down or abandonment of these projects under New Labour, this environmental activism partially ran out of steam in favor of marches during the initial terms in office.

Direct action has not completely disappeared from British social movements, but the causes that provoke it have changed. Since 1997 the nonviolent direct action movement has refocused on alter-globalism and social justice.[32] Unlike international associations or the organizers of large demonstrations, these groups are not so much seeking media attention as the possibility for their members to select their targets in accordance with their personal interests.[33] In a sense these small-scale forms of collective action occur thanks to a particular conception of the role and responsibilities of the individual in politics. They make it possible to express and articulate an identity and offer the most radical elements a way of intervening personally and directly on the political stage.

Order and Security: "Cruel Britannia"

From his first speech as a Labour leader in 1993, Tony Blair made security a major priority. His government kept this promise; more than fifty laws were adopted on security issues in ten years.

The terrorist threat provided New Labour with the justification it required for a security offensive. The old Labour Party was not known for excessive liberalism. On the contrary, the Attlee and Wilson governments had been moderately on the side of law and order, in touch with the workerist tradition of the party, sometimes tinged with moralism for the popular classes. However, the subject was not a central one for Labour.

Things changed in the 1980s when the left wing of the party attacked the police for their racism, their methods, and their involvement in Northern Ireland. It was the Thatcher government that initiated a major turn in public policy on justice and security. In this area, as in others, it took its inspiration from the American experience and toughened laws in a punitive direction, while the police were supported unstintingly in financial terms. When the Conservatives became weaker under the leadership of John Major, its only popular policies were those of maintaining law and order and challenging the rights of immigrants and asylum-seekers. Thanks to repressive legislation, the home secretary, Michael Howard, became the hero of the "nasty party."[34]

Labour mobilized against the use of the police during major industrial conflicts (the miners' strike), and botched investigations resulting in the conviction of young blacks. The police were identified with Conservative policies to such an extent that, by contrast, Labour seemed like an antipolice party. However, in 1992 the new Labour leader, John Smith, gave the portfolio of home secretary in the shadow cabinet (the opposition team that replies to the government) to the young Tony Blair (whose nickname at the time was Bambi, on account of his youthful looks). Blair broke with his party's policies. Conscious of the danger of allowing the Conservatives to appropriate the theme of security, he soon changed Labour attitudes and dispensed with what he regarded as left-wing shibboleths. His slogan—"Tough on crime and tough on the causes of crime"—enjoyed great success: the time of excuses for criminals was over. Adopting the rhetoric of American communitarians (Hale, 2006), he emphasized individual responsibility without abandoning social issues. In an interview for the homeless' magazine, *The Big Issue*, that has remained famous, Blair thus declared in January 1997 in the run-up to the election that he believed in "zero-tolerance policy against beggars" because of the "chain of association between begging, homelessness and petty crime," and never gave to mendicants. He added: "It is right to be intolerant of people homeless on the streets."[35]

After a decade of government, in the area of security, as in so many others, there was a lively debate over achievements. New Labour was attacked by the popular press for its alleged laxity. The popularity of initiatives in the struggle against insecurity persuaded the government to adopt an ever more openly illiberal rhetoric and policy, prompting the mobilization of groups to defend basic British freedoms against the state's authoritarian drift.[36]

Thus, even before the New York attacks of 11 September 2001, the Blair government worked to strengthen the ability of the state apparatus to react to the terrorist threat. Where once Britain had been famous for its liberalism, and sometimes criticized by its neighbors (including France) for its toleration of political groups linked to extremist circles, the Blair governments considerably strengthened special police powers as early as 2000. From 2001 this theme became central, and three laws radically transformed the conditions of policing and justice in Britain.[37] A law of 2001 authorized the government to opt out of the European Convention, which had only just been ratified, allowing it to detain indefinitely any foreign national suspected (but not convicted) of links with terrorist circles. These measures, which were immediately implemented, provoked an outcry from lawyers and an ongoing conflict between the highest judicial authorities—the judges appointed to the House of Lords who serve as the last instance of appeal (the Law Lords)—and the government.[38]

The introduction of computerized identity cards also conflicts with the liberal tradition and increases distrust of state control. The affair may seem banal when seen from France, where an ID card has existed since 1921. However, it is less so in view of the use that has been made of different data files in Britain. In the absence of a computer and liberties commission (the French CNIL, Commission Nationale Informatique et Libertés), systematic sharing of data is carried out by insurance companies, banks, the police, and no doubt the National Health Service (assuming that its system works one day).[39] New Labour's enthusiasm for new technology has made some highly private data accessible. In the context of antiterrorism laws, a whole set of breaches of privacy have been legalized, without any need for requests for authorization.

The new antiterrorism measures have been used in contexts wholly un-related to terrorist movements: to maintain order and to control certain groups, such as the environmentalist movement. Among the numerous pieces of legislation on the subject adopted since 1998, some, such as the 2005 law on large-scale organized crime, authorize stronger police con-trols for any "terrorist" activity. Thus, although the "animal liberation" or anti-GMO activist groups barely number more than a few dozen people, their strategy of harassing firms engaged in animal or biotechnological ex-periments was perceived as a serious economic threat, after various phar-maceutical groups had threatened to relocate their activities. The law was also used, in particular, to restrict demonstrations in the vicinity of Parlia-ment.[40]

After the London attacks of July 2005, the resources at the disposal of in-vestigators were increased and the antiterrorism struggle became central—some would even say obsessive. Several attacks were thwarted at the last minute and terrorist networks or cells dismantled. There is no doubt that, if threats to security increase, the state must defend its citizens by upgrad-ing its means of action. But the question remains: how far can the defense of democracy justify jeopardizing democracy and its operation? Labour's narrow victory in the spring 2005 elections (they retained a majority but lost a large number of MPs) illustrates the unease about a government that multiplied emergency powers, while demanding trust and promising to make a moderate use of them. Parliament imposed a limit of twenty-eight days on the period for which the police could hold a suspect without charge (the home secretary had demanded ninety),[41] but various cases of abusive detention have already been exposed.

Surveillance and the Maintenance of Order

Tony Blair always defended the idea that security is a fundamental right, particularly for the popular classes. Having invested a lot in this area to neutralize the Conservatives, New Labour made maintaining order its priority. As early as 1998, a major law on public disorder and crime asserted the principle of the struggle against antisocial behavior and partnership between neighborhood associations, local authorities, and the forces of law and order. Policing was not spared the bureaucratic revolution;[42] it even flourished, because the development of information systems multiplied opportunities for control and surveillance, while concern with performance prompted the government to reduce delays in the justice system by abolishing various possibilities open to the defense.

One after another, successive home secretaries increased police powers and displayed a veritable fascination with new technologies. The rationalization of this sector translated into a massive use of new surveillance tools, which reinforced the impression that "Big Brother is watching you."[43] Britain in fact holds the record for the number of surveillance cameras (in both public and private places). Their number was estimated at 1 million in 2003 and 4.2 million in 2007 (that is, one camera for every fourteen inhabitants). On average, they take three hundred images a day of each individual (civil and individual liberties activists now target them).[44] Furthermore, public services have been allowed to share computer files in order to track fraud and profiteers from social benefits. The British Information Commissioner's Office became concerned in 2007 about this proliferation, noting that Britain had become the most highly monitored Western country and that infringements of private life were on the rise. But the progression has not been halted. In April 2007 the British press echoed a major advance promoted by the home secretary—cameras that talk via the intermediary of surveillance agents in a child's voice, maximizing the surprise effect. The chap who drops a piece of paper on the ground or two people who are fighting can now be reprimanded live!

The multiplication of computer data (ranging from commuter train season tickets to future electronic identity cards, or the creation of DNA data banks in the framework of police investigations) is supposed to ensure the

effectiveness of police operations in tracking of organized crime and terrorists. However, since the measures that infringe private life are to be feared
"only if you've got something to hide," all controls are justified in advance.
In New Labour's Britain surveillance is justified on the grounds sometimes
of the terrorist threat, sometimes of the efficiency of public services, and
sometimes by the innocuousness of transparency for those with nothing to
hide.

Zero Tolerance

The combination of policies of surveillance and repression (as well as the
growth in antisocial behavior and crime) massively increased the rate of incarceration, despite regular measures to develop alternatives to prison. The
figure of 65,000 prisoners reached under the Conservatives appeared to be
proof of their social failure at the time. With more than 80,000 behind bars,
Britain now holds the European record. The rate of imprisonment is 1.5
times that of France or Germany, but remains one-fifth that of the United
States. Figures of this magnitude have encouraged subcontracting: 10 of the
139 British prisons are under contract to private firms (covering 8 percent
of prisoners). One of them—a model of efficiency—reduced workforce
costs drastically and prisoners had to follow orders given by loudspeakers:
a blissful impersonal world! A wave of suicides put an end to that experiment.

However, without shouting it from the rooftops, home secretaries also
took a second look at the harshest aspects of the Conservative program,
such as the policy of "zero tolerance." Private prisons were partially called
into question. Behind the rhetoric of law and order, New Labour did not
ignore the principles of rehabilitation and follow-up care. Courts have had
greater resources available to them to support the families of delinquent
minors and help young people and first-time offenders. The probation system has been reformed, and the aid budget for reintegration doubled. The
government also invested significant resources in the development of pris-
oner education. While the individual responsibility of criminals was always
given priority, ministers underlined the impact of the disintegration of local communities and families. In order to limit the number of prisoners,

the government encouraged shorter sentences combined with community work.

For the Blairites the counterpart of rights and the logic of choice is taking individual responsibility. Blair and his ministers did not hesitate to resort sometimes to incentives and sometimes to coercion. Nor did they hesitate to use a populist rhetoric demonizing certain groups, or to adopt more punitive measures in order to maximize the media impact. The murder of a little boy by two children under the age of ten allowed them, for example, to call into question the absence of criminal responsibility for the under-thirteens. Also striking was the decision to make parents responsible.

Since 1998 various financial penalties have been assessed for parents whose children commit illegal acts or play hooky. Locally, curfews were introduced for minors. The aim of this program, with its often moralizing accents, was to compel families to behave "properly." This desire for social control led to the creation of ASBOs (Anti-Social Behaviour Orders), which made it possible to exclude an individual from a neighborhood or community. For the government it involved encouraging local groups to take control of the issue of security in streets and neighborhoods, in partnership with the police and local authorities. The purpose of ASBOs is to remove individuals, heads of gangs, drug-sellers, violent husbands or fathers, down-and-outs, and alcoholics who represent a threat to public order.[45] The dangers of such a program, regarded by Tony Blair as a symbol of New Labour's effectiveness in the fight against crime, are clear. Everything depends on its implementation. Here there is no defense or trial; we are dealing with a discretionary measure. The rhetoric of law and order in the local community can soon degenerate into the exclusion of individuals who are nonconformist or whose morality poses a problem for the right-thinking people of a street or a neighborhood. The risks of drift are considerable and legal safeguards nonexistent. Whereas the use of ASBOs was initially very moderate (around five hundred in the first five years), Tony Blair chose to reinforce the moralistic, "communitarian" approach during his second mandate. The "Respect" program, already more punitive than its predecessors, was accompanied by a panoply of repressive bills. The Anti-Social Behaviour Act (2004) makes it possible, in particular, to inflict financial or penal sanctions on the parents of deviant adolescents. At the same time use of ASBOs was extended, and around five thousand were issued.

Movements defending civil liberties denounced the systematic criminalization of antisocial behavior: a 2001 law provided for fines for a number of minor infringements (crossing a railway line, being drunk in a public place, or being disrespectful toward the police). The accumulation of these penalties progressively criminalized part of the poor population, and massively criminalized young people from ethnic minorities in problem neighborhoods, which changes in penal policy were seeking to rehabilitate. The stigmatization of a minority regarded as antisocial justifies accusations of "punitive populism." This reactionary drift was all the more disquieting in that fears of terrorism encouraged occasional disturbing short-cuts.

Is New Labour's record democratic and progressive, or manipulative and authoritarian? A little bit of each at once. While some unquestionable advances were made in terms of rights and equality of opportunity, the democratization of the United Kingdom could well turn out to be an illusion if collective action gives way to punctual, private intervention, which is likely to vary depending on the success of marketing operations by the promoters of causes. Marked by tensions internal to the party, the New Labour elites sought to apply to the country recipes that had allowed them to seize the initiative in their own organization. Convinced that they were enlightened by systematic recourse to the latest studies and performance indicators, the Blair governments were largely insensitive to the demands articulated by those who challenged their actions. When communications efforts proved insufficient, consultation procedures could at least provide an illusion of participation. As regards security, New Labour above all distinguished itself from the more left wing period in the party's history, adopting certain traditional Labour themes but within a framework inherited from the Conservative governments. British political life and civil society have been profoundly transformed by the New Labour governments, because the new tools of governance have accelerated processes of individualization and deepened the crisis of representative institutions in the Westminster system.

In an important essay on postdemocracy drawn from the Italian and

British experiences in particular, Colin Crouch (2004) pondered two democracies led by internationalized social groups governing with advanced marketing techniques in the name of democracy, strengthening the security apparatus to confront social tensions that are inevitable in a society organized by market mechanisms, and systematically calling into question the institutions of representative democracy and intermediate bodies. Developments in the delivery of public policy in the course of Tony Blair's third term were clearly a step in that direction.

Conclusion: Toward a Market Society

Les histoires d'amour, comme les histoires politiques, finissent mal, en général. Like love stories, stories of political leaders have sad endings. Once the little prince of Labour's political renewal, Tony Blair surpassed historical records of unpopularity as he celebrated ten years in government in May 2007. The British people had rarely had so little trust in their prime minister, who dragged behind him like a ball and chain the engagement in Iraq, abuses of slogans and press manipulation, the scandal of private financiers in the 2005 election campaign, and the overdose of announcements, objectives, and indicators in the health system.

The decade was rich in change. If his long-expected departure was not as triumphant as he might have wished, there is scarcely any doubt that Tony Blair proved himself a peerless politician—determined, courageous, and convinced of his mission. As he put it in 2005, "[G]overnment is not a state of office but a state of mind. A willingness to accept the burden of true leadership."

In our introduction we referred to the issues of the overall assessment of the New Labour decade and its interpretation. We analyzed New Labour on the basis of public policy implementation and changes in the party and in relations with citizens, while taking account of the dynamics over ten years. Some points in the record are clear, while others remain pending.

Even if New Labour retained various social objectives, its priority was to pursue the creation of what Karl Polanyi called a "market society" (Polanyi,

1957)—that is, a society in which market principles guide and constrain the behavior of organizations and individuals (Le Galès and Scott, 2008). In the early 1990s, John Major, the conservative successor to Margaret Thatcher, occasionally mentioned his dream of turning Britain into some kind of Hong Kong of Europe. Tony Blair himself was said to be a great admirer of Singapore, its interventionist state, its safe heaven for international capital, and the authoritarian control of its citizens.

New Labour was not socialist: that much is clear. Like social democrats, it was concerned with the organization of society, social engineering and control, but also with technology. It accepted the market economy. However, the Thatcher legacy left its mark. In the case of Tony Blair in particular, the choices of citizen-consumers and competition mechanisms were always at the forefront, without any critical distance. The introduction of market mechanisms has unquestionably had positive effects on dynamism and improved efficiency in some areas—in the school system, for instance. However, the opposite proved also true in a great number of other areas, health or housing, for instance. Every regulatory mechanism has its limits, be it the state, the market, reciprocity, or large-scale organization. Obsessed with globalization and the desire to differentiate itself from the old Labour Party, New Labour lost any critical sense, even of the most moderate variety, about the market and its potentially perverse or unanticipated effects on society.

British society is harsh, and ten years of Blair governments consolidated that aspect of it. In principle, a society that is mainly regulated by market mechanisms is a society that exerts pressure on individuals, that creates more marked inequalities and social tensions. Karl Polanyi and Max Weber, who were no radicals, have shown how, in general, the market is involved in the destruction of traditional social structures, social solidarities, and institutions. By encouraging actors to behave efficiently as egoistic, rational actors, market mechanisms may destroy the normative foundations of institutions and collective action. The state can help to create these foundations, to introduce and maintain a set of rules that constitute the parameters within which market mechanisms generate their effects. In a market system, actors are in principle supposed not to obey orders but to pursue their individual interests. This poses the problem of the social stability of such societies. How can the predictability of actions and their results be guaranteed, when actors are not constrained by loyalty within a stable, predictable environment?

The answer lies in bureaucracy, rules, and penalties. For more than ten years, in the wake of Mrs. Thatcher, New Labour participated in the political construction of a market society in Britain by mobilizing the state apparatus. From the perspective of social science, it is thus perfectly logical to perceive more social tension, more crime, more antisocial behavior, justifying reinforcement of the state's role. Britain is a hybrid political and social model, a cross between the United States and the major countries of Western Europe. Colin Crouch (2008) coined the phrase "private Keynesianism" to describe the cycle of economic growth engineered by the house price boom and a mountain of private debt. Private debt is essential in the making of the market society, and the government actively supported the banks in loaning money to buy houses. The changing system for financing higher education (increased fees and the near abolition of grants for students, thus replaced by bank loans) has indeed led to the making of a generation of students leaving university with significant debt . . . in the expectation of making them more "rational" actors on the labor market.

For New Labour, those who govern in the context of globalization must analyze the issues and provide technical, technological, or managerial solutions. The state itself must adapt to the new structures of globalized capitalism and the emergent society. New Labour pushed the notion of the electoral mandate (binding the winning party to its election promises) to its extreme,[1] making it a criterion for assessing the performance of the governing class. At the price of intensive bureaucratic rationalization, the prime minister and his chancellor of the exchequer asserted their capacity for initiative and control. But this development reflected a conception of the state as service "provider," or at least as guarantor of public service provision, via the rules that it establishes and changes—that is, a state which is at once activist and regulatory, but also characterized by light regulation upon the City in order to foster financial prosperity.

The models of neoclassical microeconomics, and the postulate of the rational instrumental actor, were never questioned by New Labour; it even reinforced them with a theoretical foundation inherited from Thatcherism. This view of human nature has immediate implications for political action; it inspired the development of new public policy instruments and, in particular, an enthusiasm for controls and for creating new systems of rewards and penalties for individual actors. At the same time, it helps to explain New Labour's difficulties in resolving certain crises, or even in understanding the aberrations of some of their reforms, such as the increasing overcrowding in transport, problems in the health sector despite investment, or the challenge of climate change. These presuppositions guided the choice of instruments and interlocutors. The government used individual incentives and penalties; it addressed itself mainly to private actors, firms, associations, or individuals.

The party itself was the first target of modernizing efforts by the forces of New Labour. The changes made to it foreshadowed the social reforms, and especially the hesitation and pragmatism. Taking control of the party was no mere cosmetic operation: the internal culture was the object of much attention, so that policy proposals—most of which were modified before the election of Tony Blair as leader in 1994—also reflected new ways of interacting and understanding the role and place of a party of government in a society in motion. The party's structures were transformed in order to increase the organization's so-called inclusivity by limiting the powers of the trade unions and activists and prioritizing members who were only marginally involved. The sovereignty of the annual conference was eroded in favor of mechanisms for constant consultation, closely dependent on government teams. The policy forums served less to consult the base than to legitimate decisions that had already been taken. The party was in the process of becoming a campaign organization, structured like a private firm and likely to subcontract a number of its operations to experts and political communications professionals.

The decisions, sometimes symbolic and sometimes spectacular, taken during the first hundred days of the first Blair government gave the impression that the party was the bearer of a fixed "project" of carefully prepared reforms. In retrospect, the three successive terms prove that this was never the case. New Labour combined significant reforms carried out with determination and projects developed without conviction or clear guidelines. In numerous cases the reforms were elaborated gropingly or guided by a few principles or pragmatic "recipes," a common feature of most governments. The activism that characterized the New Labour governments was structured by a belief in the inevitability of neoliberal economic globalization. The legacy that they found when reaching power after eighteen years of Conservative government excluded any return to the past. In fact, for Tony Blair, like Margaret Thatcher before him, there was no alternative. "I hear people say we have to stop and debate globalization. You might as well debate whether autumn should follow summer," he explained at the Labour Party conference in 2005. In a sense, the modernizers who took power in the Labour Party, and then in the country, were convinced that they were an enlightened vanguard acting in accordance with the course of history . . . well, at least until the financial crisis broke out.

Similarly, the important structural reforms that have transformed the United Kingdom are not limited to the constant restructuring of an activist state rapidly adapting to its environment. They have also profoundly affected British political culture, modes of interaction, and citizens' expectations as to their role in society and what they can expect from politicians. Visitors are struck by the profound transformation of British society. Some of these developments are the product of social engineering, whose results are not always those that had been anticipated. In fact, the governments were the victims of their own illusions: they genuinely believed that they could pilot social change with perfect precision thanks to their techniques and tools.

In line with the Conservatives, New Labour promoted a progressive individualization of relations to the political, as expressed in particular by the concept of the citizen-consumer. They contributed to a gradual erosion of trust in representative institutions, at the cost of a disengagement from traditional processes, although Britain is not the only country in this condition. They promoted the expansion of civil society and created new opportunities for "social entrepreneurs" to intervene in the public domain. They brought a new model of "democratization," forcing the opening up of old hierarchies but also reinforcing inequalities of participation. The inclusive approach that was constantly invoked as a mode of democratization is often seen as an artifice designed to legitimate decisions that had already been taken. British political life has been transformed by the calling into question of old institutions that have now virtually become obsolete. "Post-democracy," to use Colin Crouch's words (2004), is fueled by the technological illusion of virtual communication, interactivity, and the plasticity of new forms of participation. Yet the latter are minimalist and individualized. How can people mobilize for collective goods when the only legitimate model is that of egoism? The "citizen-consumer" is invested with an imaginary, quasi-magical power to influence generalized markets. He or she is also encouraged, admonished, made responsible, and inspected.

The economic and social balance sheet of New Labour is ambivalent for the same reasons: the macroeconomic results were good for ten years; growth was maintained at higher levels than those of neighbors; and significant investment was made in public services (in order to remedy decades of negligence by the Conservatives and during the first term). The cult of performance entailed the concentration of centers into hypermodern clusters with considerable resources and a degree of autonomy. A number of changes allowed for an improvement in terms of income, health, or opportunity, but the pressures increased on individuals, who were not all persuaded by the government's action. Convinced that it was misunderstood and faced with an ungrateful population, New Labour's frustration is understandable.

Institutional and constitutional reforms were a key area for the Blair governments and yet the one that seems to have presented most difficulties when it came to establishing a precise timetable. While granting important powers to the new parliaments and executives in Scotland, Wales, and Northern Ireland, New Labour sought to maintain the Westminster system and, in particular, the quasi-fusion of legislative and executive powers. Devolution therefore raises numerous questions, because it creates the possibility of intervening in other people's affairs: Scottish MPs in the Commons can vote on matters concerning education in England, thus supporting the government "South of the Border," while rejecting the application of these decisions to their own nation (thanks to financial autonomy derived from the generosity of English taxpayers). It is likely that a future government—especially if it is Conservative—will seek to resolve this contradiction. The reforms of the House of Lords and of the voting system are likewise unfinished business. New Labour's hesitations were due to their distrust when it came to electoral procedures. Blair used the powers of patronage at his disposal for the second chamber to the full and constantly sought to control the selection of Welsh and Scottish leaders and candidates. The experience of a multiparty system on the periphery, and the vote of MPs on the election of the Lords in February 2007, showed that a movement was emerging to conclude this unfinished reform after his departure.

Tony Blair was a man inspired by strong moral and religious convictions. He was convinced of the need to seize opportunities in order to transform them into a competitive advantage. During the ten years he was in charge of the United Kingdom, he constantly sought to identify and grasp those opportunities that would make it possible to modernize the country and adapt it to the constraints of a globalized economy. He displayed the same qualities (or the same zeal) in international policy and strove to spread Western political and economic values—that is, essentially, democracy (understood as individual choice in a transparent, competitive market) and human rights. This enthusiasm resulted in the military intervention in Kosovo, repeated efforts to obtain a "road-map" for peace in Palestine, and, of course, the intervention in Iraq. Many questioned Blair's seemingly voluntary servitude to George Bush. The commitment of troops alongside the Americans in the absence of a UN resolution (something that had already been the case with Kosovo) can be seen as an act of opportunism—albeit naive—or as an alignment with the positions of the international *hegemon*, or as an attempt to repeat the success obtained in Yugoslavia. In dethroning a bloody dictator, and trying by the same token to impose Western freedoms in the Middle East, Blair no doubt hoped that a democratic Iraq could serve as a model for its neighbors. He was half able to convince his fellow citizens by invoking his good faith and absolute certainty, but this personalization of power and constant invocation of trust doubtless explains the disillusionment of the British people and their growing cynicism.

Whereas the rhetoric of the Conservative years constantly counterposed Europe to the United Kingdom, Tony Blair's arrival in Downing Street marked the beginning of a new phase of British involvement in the institutions of the European Union. New Labour intended to break with the policy of the empty chair and confront the thorny issue of joining the euro. However, Blair's record in this area was strangely modest, in part because his ambitions were nibbled away by the prudence of his chancellor. Tony Blair promised a referendum on giving up the pound sterling, but its organization was made conditional on the satisfaction of economic convergence criteria that were entirely under the control of the skeptic Gordon Brown. Nevertheless, we should not ignore an instrumentalist approach to Europe. Fervent defender of enlargement to the east, Blair no doubt regarded these new developments as a chance not only to ensure the unity and pacification of the Continent but also to dilute the influence of his major rivals (in particular, France and Germany). Finally, New Labour's Europeanism was evangelical: the British hoped to convince others of the inevitability of reforms and adaptation to the harsh reality of neoliberal globalization. Delays in adopting the single currency also served the interests of domestic politics: they made it possible to maintain the divisions in the Conservative Party. Thus, the latter focused the 2001 election campaign on safeguarding the national currency (a secondary issue for voters), conceding the themes of the economy and public services to New Labour. Not content with having suffered a second crushing defeat, while they were at it the Conservatives elected a new leader whose main characteristic was his ferocious opposition to Europe. A dreadful speaker, without any political flair or experience, Iain Duncan Smith was the ideal opponent for Labour. Deposed by a coup instigated by his party's elites, he was replaced in November 2003 by a former minister, Michael Howard, who was hardly any better at freeing the party from the tensions inherited from the Thatcher period. It was only in the autumn of 2005 that the Conservatives chose a young leader—David Cameron—excellent with the media, capable of threatening New Labour's dominance, and who pushed imitation of New Labour to the point of forming a duo for renewing the Conservative Party with his friend and accomplice (and one day hostile brother?) George Osborne. Since 2007,

Gordon Brown has had to deal with the wearing effect of power, but also with a more combative opponent mimicking Blair at times to promote "a new—what else?—Conservative party."

Under New Labour guidance, Britain has become more like a "market society" and has also moved toward the "post-democracy" model, deeply eroding the collective sense and purpose. At the same time it has become a more open society, exporting more capital, tourists, and pensioners, but also welcoming large numbers of migrants, students . . . and financial flux. The language of equality has disappeared in the pursuit of an ideal society where "[n]ot . . . all succeed equally—that is utopia; but an opportunity society where all have an equal chance to succeed" (Blair, 2004). The New Labour society is a meritocratic society, geared toward the needs and the priorities of middle classes, but also an inclusive society in which the issue of social justice is bound up with individual effort and brownie points are accumulated thanks to an ability to make the "right" choices. Thus, liberalization is accompanied by greater risks of penalty in case of error, failure, or deviance. The levity of "Cool Britannia" has been transformed into an impossible dual constraint: "Be spontaneous," but also "be transparent" in the name of efficiency and security.

As in the case of Margaret Thatcher, the Blair legacy also depends on the dissemination of his ideas. The Third Way featured as a vanishing star of political theory, but the transformation of political priorities and public policy tools created fear, respect, and envy in different parts of Europe . . . until the economic crisis brought in a devastating blow. In France the presidential candidate Nicolas Sarkozy borrowed many of his 2007 campaign themes, rhetoric, and promises from Tony Blair.

Postscript: The Fall of New Labour

Having plotted to do so for many years, Gordon Brown finally took over as prime minister in June 2007, smoothly endorsed by his party as the unopposed, self-evident heir to Tony Blair. There was then much hope that a key architect of the amazing first hundred days of 1997, a man who planned his promotion to the premiership for ten years and had dreamt about the position since he was a boy, would take office brimming with projects and ideas, leading Labour to a fourth term.

Two years later, our point is not to relate the ups and downs—mostly downs—of Brown's premiership, but rather to underline the exhaustion of the New Labour project and the changes that have started to emerge with the economic crisis. Several question marks remain in our assessment and are reviewed in line with the developments under the leadership of Gordon Brown.

As feared by the Blairites, the initial dynamics of the Brown government was rapidly succeeded by failures and difficulties. After a short bright spell marked by several crises, the government plunged into record unpopularity. The exhaustion of a party in power for more than a decade is one explanation, and the lack of charisma of Gordon Brown may provide another. What is more interesting, however, is to point out the extent to which the difficulties of the Brown government also proved to be the making of ten years of Brown as chancellor of the exchequer.

In other words, many problems encountered by Labour under Brown were the consequences of policies initiated during the previous decade: self-inflicted debacles, a very difficult position for the prime minister. The period of growth was fueled by massive private debt. Indeed, Britain faced serious economic difficulties such as inflation, rocketing housing prices, low productivity, and a fading growth before the financial crisis exploded. The golden rule of public investment was broken and public debt started to rise beyond 40 percent of GDP (but from a sound base), while massive household debt fueled a consumption boom financed by the banks. Rising inequalities, a hospital crisis, and a school exams crisis were all linked to decisions made a few years before.

The collapse in 2007 of the Newcastle-based bank Northern Rock, in the middle of the Labour heartland, also demonstrated the lack of effectiveness of financial regulations . . . nearly a year before the global financial crisis. Northern Rock specialized in housing and was active in "refinancing" mortgages, lending up to 125 percent of the price of a property. "Releasing equity" had become a giant lottery game to release cash and to increase massive private debt. In 2007 private debt in the UK became greater than the GDP (that's not to mention public debt) and fed the property boom, which encouraged more "remortgaging." Used to an environment of sustainable growth and probably believing that its reforms would lead to long-term growth, Brown did not read the warnings that accumulated in the aftermath of the Northern Rock collapse.

The steady rise in prices for homes and the increase in private debt have been pivotal for the economic growth enjoyed by Britain under New Labour. However, housing can be seen as a crucial policy failure for other reasons than its ultimate weakening of the UK's economic stability. During the years of property boom, the construction of new housing remained a low priority. Sky-rocketing prices and a shortage of housing reached a climax in London, where the super rich broke new records with ostentatious properties. By the end of the Blair years, the average price of a British house was about five times the average wage. The situation worsened particularly for the most disadvantaged groups, and the undersupply of social housing reached a crisis point. The Barker Report on housing supply (2004)[1] estimated that the number of people on local authority's housing waiting lists has increased by 73 percent between 1997 and 2007.

Housing was given a higher priority under Brown, with the publication of a green paper on the provision of affordable and sustainable homes in July 2007. But questions remain: the ambitious new plans have been designed to build housing in the East of London; the advent of the economic and financial crisis is slowing down construction because housing associations (which are not-for-profit organizations) can no longer raise private capital, and local authorities are now allowed to build barely more than insignificant numbers. While the goal is to provide 3 million new homes by 2020, estimates give the figure of only eighty thousand new houses available for the year 2009.

The New Labour credo has been that growth and market efficacy would bring social justice, and that individuals should be either enticed or forced to adapt to economic "reality." In charge of Work and Pension, the young Blairite James Purnell kept the New Labour line on social policy under Brown. He introduced more pressure for those seeking jobs, from single mothers with children to various kinds of disabled. He came out with ambitious plans to turn the screw once more. He created more "incentives" but above all more penalties for those remaining outside the active labor market. Struggling to find a home, pressured by unforgiving market forces, the British poor have found little comfort in the social policies of the successive New Labour governments.

Brown's record on redistribution has been tainted by several heavily challenged attempts at reforming the tax system. In 2007, the introduction at the last minute of a tax evasion scheme for inheritance in the budget bore witness to the abandonment of any attempt for more progressive distribution. The reform had been advocated by the Conservatives for a long time. A year later, a new tax reform that hit the lowest paid workers provoked a backbench rebellion that was barely avoided thanks to the ingenuity of Chancellor Alistair Darling's invention of a compensating scheme. Only in 2009, one year into the crisis, the introduction of a new tax bracket for the super rich hints at Labour's reconnecting with its traditional base. Indeed, inequalities have not decreased under New Labour but are, on the contrary, becoming more blatant, and Labour's symbolic promise to halve the rate of children in poverty by 2010 is not going to be fulfilled (improvement by a third is likely to take place). Some of the most progressive policies introduced during the New Labour years, such as the minimum wage or Sure Start, are unlikely to survive the economic crisis or the likely change of government, because they were introduced in the name of market efficacy rather than social justice and moral obligation.

The massive investments undertaken after 2000 have led to a partial renewal of basic infrastructures that were crucially needed. They have been particularly important in education, research, and health, and they have contributed to an important rise in public sector employment. However, all this did not lead to British public services becoming cutting edge in Europe, nor did it fundamentally change their image. The "bureaucratic revolution" that accompanied it was more than rhetorical, but after more than a decade of change, appetite for a further thrust of public service reform has dissipated. Gordon Brown has neither Blair's reforming courage nor his political good luck; he has accepted reluctantly a number of policy U-turns (on ID cards, the privatization of Royal Mail, the nationalization of the East-coast rail services). Despite the failed attempt by the government to increase the number of days in detention without charges, the overall orientation of illiberal social policies and control remains clear under the premiership of Gordon Brown.

The widely welcomed publication of the Stern Report on climate change in late 2006,[2] and the growing popularity of the issue in the British media, have no doubt contributed to a greening of governmental discourse. The report has inspired creative plans and new sets of targets. However, the Brown government's record tends to show that Britain is lagging behind other major developed countries in the implementation of "green" policies. It is unlikely to meet its own legally binding targets of an 80 percent cut in CO_2 emissions by 2050 (and a 34 percent cut by 2020) because most of its programs are either behind schedule (such as the development of renewable energy) or abandoned (such as the plan to make all new homes be carbon-neutral by 2016 and the objective of improving the energy efficiency of existing housing stock); it is clinging to old policy dogmas and pressure groups. For instance, and despite public protest, it is expanding airports and motorways while bailing out the car industry.

New Labour had been elected with the promise to restore faith in the political process and to bring back honesty to Westminster after the sleaze scandals of the latter Conservative years, but cynicism grew under Tony Blair's premiership because the news spin cycle and the lies associated with the war in Iraq further undermined public trust in politicians and political institutions. Brown's lack of charisma made politics less slick, and his first speech as prime minister even struck as refreshingly uninspired. For a while, his dour style happily contrasted with the charm of the reviled Blair. However, what at first sight was taken as an eagerness to "get on with the job of governing" progressively became a symptom of Brown's inability to fix the problems he had contributed to create as chancellor. He proved unable or unwilling to invent new recipes for governing and clung to the targets and performance indicators that had lost credence within the public. Competent young ministers enumerating endless performance indicators to convince everybody of the greatness and effectiveness of New Labour achievements being treated with absolute cynicism by their audience has become a classic scene of British politics.

In other words, Brown may have dropped the adjective "new" from the moment he endeavored to replace Tony Blair as prime minister and sought to build his strategy on his networks within the old party, but under his leadership there has been very little that was new or that was not following the New Labour faith in the supreme efficacy of the market model. Almost from day one the Brown government looked politically exhausted, with no further idea than to keep the New Labour project on tracks.

Devolution: From British Politics to National Arenas

Beyond domestic policy difficulties, devolution is also proving to be a difficult legacy. Firstly, politics in both Scotland and Wales has become more and more differentiated from that of London and England. In Wales, as one would have expected, the powers initially granted to the devolved institutions had given Welsh politics a distinctively more traditional Labour flavor. After several years of pressure, Welsh premier Rhodri Morgan obtained a new Welsh Act, paving the way for more autonomy and increasing the limited powers of the Welsh Assembly.

Welsh politics has progressively become very distinct, with no dominant party. In the Welsh Assembly elected in May 2007, Labour won 26 seats, the pro-independence party Plaid Cymru 15, the Conservatives 12, the Liberal Democrats 6, and there is one independent. On 7 July 2007, Plaid Cymru signed an agreement with Labour to be part of the governing coalition. Such an agreement may not seem extraordinary in most European countries, but it represents a striking innovation in the UK context and it made little sense in British—that is, English—politics. The impact on regional public policy has been striking, as the Welsh executive has since not only consistently resisted market pressures but also consolidated classic provision of services by local authorities.

Wales is not the only region where nationalists are on the rise. Similar developments can be seen in both Ireland and Scotland. In Scotland, the rejection of Tony Blair and of New Labour policies fed a spectacular rise of the Scottish National Party (SNP). What is the future of the Union? Will Scotland vote for independence? Devolution was supposed to give autonomy to the Scottish and restore enthusiasm for the 1707 Union with England. The SNP won in the same May 2007 regional election and became the first party in the Scottish Assembly. Alex Salmond, the nationalists' leader, became first minister of Scotland with a minority government. He immediately looked into organizing a referendum on independence despite a lack of clear parliamentary support. The prospect is provoking a major split within the Labour Party, as the leader of Scottish Labour embraced the idea of a referendum, urging an early vote with the conviction that the Union would score a resounding victory. South of the border Labour favored a more cautious approach. Plans are now delayed until 2010.

Again, the differentiation of Scottish politics is striking. Not only are the nationalists key players but the Conservatives, dominant in England, remain a marginal force there. If the electoral decline of both Labour and the Conservatives is confirmed—and whatever the limits of the nationalist movement—Scotland is fast becoming a very different political world from

England. This evolution has clear implications in terms of public policies. Scottish (and non-UK European Union) students do not pay tuition fees for higher education in Scotland,[3] and some social services are provided for free (such as school meals for pupils). The paradox is that such generous policies are partly financed by subsidies from London! The Scottish Parliament is also introducing laws that increasingly diverge from the rest of the UK, in matters such as local income tax or rules on alcohol sale and consumption. In a move similar to that of their Welsh cousins, Scottish leaders have also expressed the fiercest criticisms of the Public Private Partnership massively developed by New Labour. They have implemented instead a more classic strategy for public investments in new schools and hospitals. Serious political fights have developed between the Scottish and the UK executives about the relaunch of the nuclear power program or the decisions to stock nuclear wastes.[4]

Nationalists are in coalition governments or governing Wales, Scotland, and Northern Ireland; the Conservatives are sidelined; and the Labour Party is losing ground. If the Conservatives were to win the next general election in 2010, the gap between the Celtic periphery and London is likely to grow and to raise numerous political conflicts, fueling more nationalist demands for independence or autonomy. The economic crisis may, however, prove beneficial to the union and help diffuse some of the nationalist tensions, as small, highly internationalized economies tend to be particularly fragile. The once popular idea of transforming Scotland into a new and prosperous Iceland has somewhat lost its appeal in the aftermath of the near bankruptcy of that country.

New Labour and the Global Economic Crisis

While the 2007 conference season was dominated by speculations about anticipated general elections in the wake of the new prime minister's political honeymoon, the atmosphere a year later was drastically different. So accustomed to defend the economic miracle of the early years of New Labour, Brown was uneasy about dealing with difficulties fueled by consumption credit and the banking system. In Parliament, he faced tougher opposition than Blair ever had as the young and Blair-like Conservative leader David Cameron aggressively questioned his achievements as both former chancellor and actual prime minister. Challenges also came from the backbenches, particularly when a tax change threatened to create negative redistribution. Weakened by bad economic results, electoral defeats at the local and regional elections, severe unpopularity, bad performance in the Commons, and a nonstop drip of little government disasters (such as the loss of taxpayers' data), Brown went to the 2008 Labour conference amid speculations of plots to force a leadership contest, thereby ending his premiership. Younger colleagues in his cabinet started counting their supporters.

Surprisingly, though, after months at low ebb, the financial crisis opened a window of opportunity for Brown. Heavily criticized for his handling of the Northern Rock crisis in 2007 (that is, the collapse of a bank that the government had effectively nationalized), he suddenly presented himself as a wise state pragmatist with no fear of regulating the market. On the international scene, he was the political leader with the experience and the judgment to weather the storm. In the middle of the gigantic chaos created by financial markets, Brown acted decisively to bail out the rotten bank system (at an overall cost to the public purse of about £20 billion, so far) with de facto nationalization of several banks (most notably the once aggressive Royal Bank of Scotland). He also introduced a decrease of the VAT to support consumption and opted to create a massive public deficit in order to overcome the crisis. Breaking the golden rules set out by Brown the chancellor,[5] Brown the prime minister condoned a deficit of 12.5 percent of GDP—probably more in 2010. The national debt is now close to 50 percent, and economic forecasts plan a rapid growth in the next three years toward 80 percent of GDP. Brown and his government have justified high spending and state intervention, as in the old Labour days. Spectacularly, the government has accepted taxing the very rich, increasing tax and insurance for the 1 percent of the richest, criticizing extravagant salaries for top managers, advocating for social redistribution—and even mentioning that something should be done about tax haven! For the first time under New Labour, some level of redistribution is more decisively taking place.

Party activists had welcomed Gordon Brown's takeover of the leadership. They had hoped that he would reconnect the government with its grassroots and change tone as well as content. Many believed his rhetoric about Labour, rather than New Labour. Over the months, most had been disappointed as few policy directions changed. The explosive and directive personality of the prime minister earned him the nickname "Staline"; the succession of political gaffes, mini crises, and PR scandals turned him into "Mr Bean." However, in the context of the financial crisis, the 2008 Manchester conference restored his tarnished image. In his keynote speech, he abandoned the orthodoxy of the previous years and promised to strengthen the role of the state, including a sharp criticism of the banking industry. He said: "Just as those who supported the dogma of big government were proved wrong, so, too, those who argue for the dogma of unbridled free-market forces have been proved wrong again." The New Labour project was over. In other words, after eighteen months in office in which Brown mostly pursued a New Labour agenda in a less political and more managerial way, the financial crisis gave him the opportunity to reinvent himself, not as a leftist but as a serious social democrat who believes in direct state intervention in the market. His international success with the G20 summit allowed him to entertain the thought that he had saved the world.[6]

At the same time, Gordon Brown rediscovered Europe. A well-known Euro-skeptic with little interest or sympathy for the Continent, Brown was happy to be seen as an example by European governments. He was not shy to explain to European leaders that they had to increase the flexibility of the labor market, and to cut public expenditure, state intervention, and public services. However, the worsening of the crisis and the persistent difficulties of the UK economy (not alone of course) have led Brown for the first time to give clear indication that the EU might be important in solving the crisis, and that the UK had to be more central to the European project. Until then, Brown had been interested in the global role of the UK and had shown numerous signs of lack of interest in the EU, leading to his marginalization among EU leaders.

The Party: What Happens to New Labour ?

Ultimately, his handling of the financial crisis saved him from a leadership contest, but, although Brown's Labour government can legitimately argue that the crisis is global, Britain appears harder hit than other European economies. As months went by and the aura of the saving of the banking system faded, Brown fell back onto his New Labour creed in order to manage the economic crisis. By spring 2009 unemployment had passed the 2 million mark, and ministers were fearing the 3 million figure before the end of the year. In 2008, the government worked on a scheme aiming at providing private sector logic within the public sector. It planned to fund private firms to find jobs for the unemployed in competition with classic Job Centres. As the government was prepared to announce large contracts to private companies, early in 2009 the latter required massive grants because of the difficulty of the labor market. Private firms knew that they had no chance of reaching negotiated targets at a time of exploding unemployment. Within a shrinking labor market they were unlikely to demonstrate healthy figures in terms of bringing the unemployed back to work. As we can see, despite the change in rhetoric about regulation and state intervention, the government still harbors faith in the New Labour attempt to pursue the progressive privatization of the welfare state and to outsource an ever-growing part of what remains of the public sector. A series of policy announcements (including the privatization of the Post Office) are stirring internal party opposition once again, and Labour is wondering whether a change of leadership and direction provides any hope of avoiding an electoral massacre at the next general election.

During the two years of the Brown government the question "What is to be done?" has been sharply raised but not really answered within the party. Should the pursuit of the Blairites' radical reformist agenda be the priority? Or should Labour gravitate toward a "Continental" European left? Include a dash of Scandinavian social-democracy? Definitively turn its back on the Labour tradition and transform itself into an Italian-style democratic left, or a Democratic Party à la Clinton?; an Anglo-Saxon liberal left of the sort found in Australia and New Zealand?

When Blair went, there was no proper challenge within the Labour Party. Despite the reluctance of New Labour big beasts such as Charles Clarke, Stephen Byers, or Alan Milburn, and the hesitations of David Miliband and Alan Johnson, Gordon Brown was elected unopposed. By contrast, and as the long-serving symbol of the working class, John Prescott also went as deputy leader; the election for Brown's deputy within the party gave rise to heated debates and close results between Harriet Harman, John Cruddas from the Labour left, and Hilary Benn. Harriet Harman is married to a prominent trade union leader and was the voice of gender and equality issues. Blairites have become less distinctive as a group. However, they still appeared as more willing to introduce market mechanisms and more systematically opposed to, and by, trade unions. The young Blairite guard, such as David Miliband or James Purnell,[7] both appointed to prominent positions within Brown's cabinet, did not, however, articulate a different kind of Labour Party.

Thus, the Brown government did not seem to change much from the directions taken by former Blair governments: there was no distinctive social democrat flavor to it. There were not many new ideas either. Both during the debates within the Labour Party and in government, the Brown government did not appear to come out with anything else than what had been done before, and new managerial solutions to solve yet another health or school crisis. In other words, the Brown government has shown to many the exhaustion of the New Labour project. But if the "New Labour labeling" has been progressively abandoned and the leadership has come back to a more classic language about the "Labour" party, the evolution is linguistic rather than practical. Efforts to rebuild the organization and reconnect with drifting supporters follows the same uninspired recipes that have failed to stop the hemorrhage of members and activists. As he took over the party in 2007, Brown merely announced a new initiative to "democratize" the party through more consultative exercises. Within the party, the only change came from the reconstitution of a left wing supported by more vocal trade unions upset by the lack of support from Brown. Activists feel let down by their elite, betrayed by those who have succumbed to the sirens of easy money and power.

What is happening to New Labour? What is the Labour Party going to become? Since the time that Brown took over with his group (Ed Ball, Douglas Alexander, Ed Miliband, Jacqui Smith, Nick Brown, Yvette Cooper), the question has not been answered. Signs are difficult to read. In October 2008, the comeback of Peter Mandelson, former "Prince of Darkness" from the heyday of New Labour, former best friend and worst enemy of Brown, former European commissioner, created an interesting paradox: as Brown seemed to repudiate the free market dogma of the previous years, he welcomed the person most attached to the idea of New Labour. In the few months since his return to the front stage of British politics, the new Lord Mandelson, trade secretary and second in command after the prime minister, has had more than one opportunity to hold together what appears to be the sinking ship of the Labour government.

Spring 2009 saw a new series of calamities befall Gordon Brown. The scandal of MPs from all parties claiming reimbursement for secondary homes, already paid mortgages, porn video rentals, and duck islands hit indiscriminately all parliamentary parties, but the Conservatives were the quickest to react. While Cameron acted decisively to punish offending Tory MPs, Brown was unable to successfully quail the crisis. Politicians of all sides lost the little credibility they still had in the eyes of the public, and the consequences for the future of British politics should not be underestimated. Trust and respect for political institutions have collapsed. Once more, Brown's leadership seemed doomed as conflict erupted within the government, leading to the resignation of several ministers, including Hazel Blears and James Purnell.[8] Rumors of plotting emerged in the press, and heavyweights condemned the leadership and tried to inflict maximum damage at a time of great vulnerability. An inevitable reshuffle demonstrated how Brown was now dependent on Mandelson, his chancellor, and a shrinking number of untarnished team of allies waiting for the best time to get the knives out. But the great survivor of British politics made it once again, and he will probably lead the party to the next general election in May 2010.

From Crises to Disaster, Catastrophe, and Debacle

If the prospect of a fourth Labour mandate appears unlikely, it is thus primarily because of the sheer political exhaustion of the new Labour project. However, one also must take into account several other factors. First, the public has become weary of change, cynical about both the motives and the ability of politicians in providing answers to pressing political and social concerns. Second, the Conservatives are, for the first time in years, beginning to recover as a credible alternative government under the leadership of the young and media friendly David Cameron. The fourth leader since the fall of John Major's government, Cameron has successfully realigned his party by adopting numerous features inspired by New Labour.

The political renewal of the Conservatives is based on a calculated media offensive and the weariness of the electorate. If Brown was welcome as a potential antidote to forecast electoral disaster under Blair's leadership, he has done little to support such a belief. The party on the ground was engaged in a precipitate decline, both in terms of membership and in terms of its presence in local politics, even before his taking over. Indeed, the 2007 regional elections revealed the Labour Party's difficulties in their former stronghold of Scotland. The 2008 local elections were disastrous for Labour, whose unpopular leader seemed to have lost grasp of domestic politics. With 24 percent of the vote, Labour had its worst local results in fifty years, losing London and fledging in its traditional bastions of the North. If 2007 was a debacle and 2008 a disaster, then the 2009 European and local elections proved to be an unfathomable catastrophe. Labour came into third place, with only 15.7 percent of the vote, against 16.5 percent for the UK Independence Party (which campaigns on taking Britain out of the European Union) and 27.7 percent for the Conservatives. Labour lost the leadership of all remaining counties in England; it arrived second behind the SNP in Scotland and the Conservatives in Wales. The British National Party (6.2 percent) for the first time sent two MEPs to Strasbourg, testifying to the collapse of Labour among the working-class electorate. British voters have fallen out of love with Labour, and opinion polls give an 18 percent lead to the Conservatives on prospective general election votes.

Whatever happens in the next general election—due at the latest in Spring 2010—the Labour team cannot avoid serious reassessment of the period, as the worst aspects of the economic crisis are also part of their own making. The belief in the superiority of market mechanisms has also been eroded. Light touch regulation of the City, which was so successful in attracting wealth to the city of London, also proved to be a disaster. Public debt and cuts in public services will be on the agenda of a future government. The New Labour project is probably dead in its original form, but the making of an alternative, which will include some of those elements, is still in progress. Young and ambitious Labour MPs are giving up on the idea of a recovery, bracing themselves for a period of opposition that will give them time to rethink their political project. A great deal of work will also be necessary on the ground, as the party's coffers are empty, seriously threatening its ability to fight an expensive campaign. Generous donors deserted after successive funding scandals. Party membership is at its lowest, and activists are demobilized and angered by the expenditure scandal and the policy mistakes. Brown's last hopes rely upon a rapid economic recovery, in time for the May 2010 election.

If Labour is exhausted ideologically, politically, and organizationally, the Conservatives are gearing up for action. David Cameron has already made ambitious promises to repair "British broken politics," to reform Parliament, to devolve power, to curb central government's power and control, and to increase human rights guarantees. How the Labour Party is going to emerge from the crisis and to prepare itself for the next decade remains to be seen. But the question goes far beyond what remains of the British center-left.

Notes and Bibliography

Notes

Introduction

1. According to incrementalism, public policy invariably changes to a limited extent, in small steps, very gradually, at the margins. But the cumulative effects can eventually produce major transformations.

2. This interpretation is based on lines also sketched out by, among others, Andrew Gamble, Colin Crouch, Patrick Dunleavy, Colin Hay, Christopher Hood, and Desmond King.

3. This financial district, heart of the British economy, is a powerful interest group. See Cassis (1987).

4. The Labour Party uncritically accepted the predemocratic British state and for several generations strove to graft democratic practices onto it. See Jones and Keating (1985).

5. By revising Clause 4 of the party constitution, which for decades was printed on membership cards and had strong symbolic connotations (see Chapter 4).

6. A reference to the title of Andrew Gamble's work on the Thatcher period (1988).

7. Tony Blair has set out his vision on many occasions: "The issue is this: do we shape [change] or does it shape us? Do we master it, or do we let it overwhelm us? That's the sole key to politics in the modern world: how to manage change. Resist it: futile; let it happen: dangerous. So—the third way—manage it." Tony Blair, speech at the University of Tübingen, 30 June 2000.

8. However, the issue of decline has haunted political debates and controversies among historians since the end of the nineteenth century.

9. The notion of social engineering refers to the idea, widely developed in Scandinavian social-democracy, that senior civil servants can transform society in a rational fashion by using public policies and controlling the effects of their implementation.

10. Manipulation of the media interpretation of their speeches and political activities has been one of the most striking characteristics of New Labour. We shall return to it in Chapter 4.

11. Rational choice authors analyze public policy as the result of choice on the part of egoistic individuals, whose instrumental rationality (in terms of interest), and cost/benefit calculation of decisions (or nondecisions) are influenced by the penalties or incentives of their environment. Individuals make choices in order to maximize their interests, their satisfaction. They have preferences (not goals) that are clear, hierarchically organized, and relatively stable. They take decisions in autonomous, rational, and coherent fashion. The key issue for public action is coordinating the interactions that cumulatively produce collective forms.

12. Paul Hirst was a major British intellectual, professor of sociology and political science at Birkbeck College, London. He died prematurely in 2003.

13. The absence of competition between the two men left open the possibility that Gordon Brown might have been preferred by the party. It fueled the rancor of the chancellor, who never got a reality check on his popularity. Similarly, he avoided a contest in 2007, depriving himself of the legitimacy of an electoral victory.

14. On the relations and dynamic between this duo, see the amusing work by the *Observer* journalist Andrew Rawnsley (2001).

15. Like Margaret Thatcher in 1990, he was pushed to resign the leadership and thus the premiership by an internal coup. He announced at the 2006 annual party conference that he would leave within a year but prolonged his stay in order to outlast the Iron Lady.

16. His mentor Roy Jenkins, former chancellor of the exchequer under Harold Wilson and president of the European Commission, left the Labour Party to found the Social Democratic Party during Labour's turn to the left in 1981.

Chapter 1

1. British growth was characterized by periods of inflationary overheating, followed by an abrupt halt, impeding economic growth.

2. On this point, see the original analysis by Jenny Anderson (2007).

3. See the debate between Colin Hay and Ben Clift in *British Journal of Political Science* 37(2) 2007: 378–82.

4. The statistical mystery of this spectacular rise has yet to be fully clarified, but maintenance of the pound sterling at a very high value counted for much.

5. The nickname given by the *Observer*'s famous economics correspondent, William Keegan, who adopted it for his book *The Prudence of Mr Gordon Brown* (Chichester: John Wiley and Sons, 2004).

6. Depoliticization has gone far beyond the sphere of finance and economy, helping the Blair governments limit their responsibility by outsourcing management and provisions of public services to a variety of organizations, experts, and committees. See Burnham (2001).

7. It made it possible to benefit from the maximum media impact.

8. Economic studies of the Organization for Economic Cooperation and Development. United Kingdom, 20 November 2005.

9. For a simple, clearly argued assessment, see the book by the journalists Polly Toynbee and David Walker (2005).

10. Precise analysis of these agencies goes beyond the scope of this work, but it is an important aspect of the regulation of the British economy.

11. The UK permitted immigration from new European Union (EU) countries in 2004, and more than a million people moved to the United Kingdom between 2004 and 2008, though many of those migrations have been temporary. See Naomi Pollard et al. (2008).

12. The employment rate in France in 2005 was 61.3 percent. See Fondation Robert-Schuman (2006).

13. The papers mocked Brown's ambition in taking himself for a Roosevelt. The New Deal was in fact the name of the program of Keynesian reflation of the economy introduced by Franklin D. Roosevelt after acceding to the U.S. presidency in 1936.

14. At the same time, the government put pressure on employers to commit themselves to lowering barriers to employment for women, young people, and

ethnic minorities. The government was highly active in combating forms of discrimination.

15. From October 2007, the minimum wage was £5.52 per hour, £4.60 for eighteen- to twenty-one-year-olds, and £3.40 for sixteen- to seventeen-year-olds.

16. For example, there was a sharp conflict when Tony Blair tried to block at the European level the rights of works councils and union participation. We shall return to this in Chapter 4.

17. Moreover, child poverty increased again in 2007. See http://news.bbc.co.uk/2/hi/uk_news/politics/6497981.stm.

18. See, in particular, the publications of the Institute for Fiscal Studies, based in London.

19. In effect, Britain wanted to become the Macao of Europe, by enticing, for example, firms based in Gibraltar. A major program was launched to create seventeen casinos, including a super-casino, which was assigned to Manchester, following, naturally, the obligatory competitive tender.

Chapter 2

1. The third sector is composed of "not for profit" organizations, which are independent of the state and benefit from voluntary work.

2. See, for example, Massey (1999). For more details, readers are referred to the review *Public Administration*, which regularly publishes research work on changes in the public sector.

3. A trend accelerated after Thatcher's third electoral victory, following the report published in 1987, *Improving Management in Government: The Next Step Initiative*.

4. For example, the National Audit Office was established in 1983.

5. Hood et al. (1999).

6. Geoff Mulgan was director of the Policy Unit at 10 Downing Street and an advisor to Gordon Brown. Founder of Demos, he has been director of the Young Foundation since 2004. Mathew Taylor, deputy general-secretary of the Labour Party from 1994 to 1997, assumed the direction of the IPPR before joining the team of advisers at Downing Street. David Miliband, former researcher at the IPPR and essential contributor to the 1997 election manifesto, became

part of the Policy Unit before being elected to Parliament in 2001. Environment secretary in the last Blair government, he became the foreign secretary in Gordon Brown's government.

7. Its clients include Monsanto and Securicor Custodial Services.

8. The core executive comprises the office of the prime minister, the Treasury, the Home Office, and interministerial organizations. See Martin Smith, *Core Executive in Britain*, Basingstoke: Macmillan, 1999.

9. This has earned Brown and Blair the kind designation of "control freaks."

10. Reporting consists in collecting precise information on the procedures, results, and resources used in preformatted information systems and immediately made available to those in charge, as in firms.

11. During the decade of the Blair governments, the number of pupils in private schools increased. Some of these academies were sponsored by religious groups. Thus, for Steve Chalke, a Baptist minister who was the founder of an academy (Oasis), churches had to reoccupy the terrain of social and public services from which they had been ejected by the Labour government after World War II. There is little difference between this approach and New Labour (and Conservative) aspirations to civic renewal and the role of the voluntary sector in public services. See Madeleine Bunting, "Leap of Faith," *The Guardian*, 31 January 2007.

12. Tuition fees were introduced in the UK in 1998 but later abolished in Scotland. As of 2008–9, English university fees were capped at about £3,000.

13. British children are among the most tested in the world. See Carnie (2003).

14. The Church now no longer renders accounts exclusively to God; it has submitted to the rituals of verification and transparency dictated by the audit culture. Subject to pressures of profitability, priests organize the raising funds (£750 million are given by parishioners each year, or some three-quarters of the budget) whose use must be justified. As a result, the management of the Church has been professionalized. The personnel recruited come from the world of private enterprise. The council of the Archbishop of Canterbury (who leads the Anglican Church under the authority of the Queen) is itself subject to a financial audit. In response to the rapid secularization of British society and the liberalization of morals, the Church has liberalized its liturgy and its clergy.

Opened up to female priests and homosexuals, it now encourages dialogue between religions and toleration of behavior that was previously regarded as deviant. Despite this, the faithful have continued to desert congregations. The number of church weddings and baptisms are in decline, to the point where the most pessimistic forecast their "disappearance" within the next sixty years. Such a failure in the strategy of modernization led a think tank to suggest in December 2006 a complete audit of the institution, in order to reflect on a new development strategy.

15. Weir and Beetham (1999). This study assesses the democratic performance of British institutions (in respect of principles of authority, accountability, responsiveness, and thirty assessment criteria).

16. Pattie et al. (2004). The conclusion of this study is that British citizenship has been transformed by the individualization of modes of political action and by the recent increase in protest potential. See Chapter 5.

17. For instance, the BBC revealed in May 2008 how universities rig their students' satisfaction evaluations in order to maintain their ranking. See http://news.bbc.co.uk/2/hi/uk_news/education/7404864.stm.

Chapter 3

1. Associated Press, "After 'Au revoir, Jacques,' EU Bids Cheerless 'Cheerio' to Tony," *International Herald Tribune*, 21 June 2007, http://www.iht.com/articles/ap/2007/06/22/europe/EU-GEN-EU-Summit-Bye-Bye-Blair.php.

2. The turnout in Wales only just reached 50 percent in 1998 and 46 percent for the elections in 1999.

3. The system combines representatives elected in constituencies through a winner takes all system and members elected on a regional basis on party lists.

4. For example, the building of new parliaments: the Edinburgh parliament (Holyrood), whose architecture is (depending on your opinion) ambitious or unsightly, cost ten times more than was budgeted for—a record!

5. Ken Livingstone is a colorful character in British politics. He was a leader of the left wing of the Labour Party when he led Greater London at the beginning of the 1980s—an instance of local government abolished by Thatcher, who made "Red Ken" her pet hate. Opposed to Blair, he was marginalized in the Labour Party but remained an MP. When Blair created the post of mayor of

London (and had one of his close collaborators in mind), Livingstone started to campaign. The party leadership excluded him in a way that was scarcely democratic, but despite everything he stood as an independent and was elected. He gradually proved himself as an administrator, and New Labour once again accepted him as one of its own. Re-elected in 2004 as the Labour candidate, he eventually lost in 2008 in a context of deep Labour unpopularity.

6. Such a reform risks calling into question the supremacy of the Commons and could therefore challenge the omnipotence of one-party governments derived from a single round of voting.

7. See, for instance, Meg Russell, "Ditch the Pantomime," *The Guardian*, November 2007, http://www.guardian.co.uk/commentisfree/2007/nov/06/ditch-thepantomime.

8. Rival of Blair in 1994, Robin Cook was appointed foreign secretary in 1997. This brilliant Scottish intellect had announced his desire to conduct an "ethical" foreign policy. He was penalized for problems in his private life by being switched to leader of the House of Commons in 2001. He then busied himself with reforming Parliament, before resigning in spectacular fashion on the eve of the intervention in Iraq. He died prematurely in 2005.

9. In fact, to be a minister in the United Kingdom you have to be a parliamentarian. Lord Falconer and Lord Irvine (who succeeded each other as lord chancellor) were both ennobled, and hence appointed to the House of Lords, before being made ministers.

10. By 2003, fractures had emerged in the consensus. Orchestrated by the left of the party, the disagreements remained largely contained to the grass-roots.

11. Attitudes toward the EU became the thorn in the side of successive Conservative leaders, all compelled to appease their more radical wing, and to beware of the emergence of a quasi-splinter group, the UK Independence Party. In 2001, for instance, the Conservatives focused their general election campaign on "saving the pound" at a time when the British public was concerned with education and the National Health Service. Euro-skeptic credentials also became a key determinant for the selection of their successive leaders. Iain Duncan Smith, the first Conservative Party leader elected by the membership, was chosen mostly for the strict anti-European positions he had taken during the last Conservative government. The party elites have followed the radicaliza-

tion of the grassroots on the matter, and although David Cameron has successfully shifted the policy focus to other issues, he made important concessions to euro-skeptics upon his election to the leadership in 2005.

12. The electoral successes of sister social democratic parties in 1997 and 1998 helped cement relations with Jospin and Schroder. More than seventy ministerial visits to each country were organized in 1999 and 2000. See Bulmer and Burch (2006): 47.

13. Tony Blair has defended on many occasions the "special relationship," for instance in a speech to the Foreign Office Conference on 7 January 2003 (http://www.direct.gov.uk). See Gamble (2004), Boyce (2005).

14. Caricatures of the prime minister as the poodle of the Bush administration echoed long-term preoccupations on both the left and the right of the political spectrum about the Americanization of Britain. See Gamble (2004): 83.

15. Until 1999, the UK was the only country not to have adopted proportional representation for the election of members of the European Parliament.

16. The reforms were so associated with the influence of the British that leftist campaigners against the French referendum on the constitutional treaty in 2005 highlighted their opposition to the "imposition" of an "Anglo-Saxon," neoliberal framework.

17. Blair's attention shifted to Spain and Italy, both part of the American-led coalition in Iraq and led by right-wing governments. One remembers how the distinction between "old" and "new" Europe was popularized after Secretary of State Donald Rumsfeld used it to criticize the lack of support of Western nations for the invasion of Iraq in 2003.

18. Blair's European ambitions have been amply covered by the press over the years. See, for instance, Patrick Wintour, "I'll Be President of Europe If You Give Me the Power—Blair. Former PM Consults Old Downing Street Allies on Campaign for New EU Role," *The Guardian*, 2 February 2008.

19. These five tests were economic harmonization, flexibility, effect on investment, on financial services, and on growth and jobs.

20. Whitehall is the area of London adjoining the Houses of Parliament, where the major departments of state, as well as 10 and 11 Downing Street (residences of the prime minister and the chancellor of the exchequer), are to be found.

21. It is reckoned that approximately 20 percent of senior administrators in the civil service have been recruited from outside its ranks, as opposed to internal promotion.

22. Expenses tripled in ten years.

23. See Andrew Rawnsley, "Just Flesh and Blood," *The Guardian*, 24 September 2000, as well as Rawnsley (2001).

24. See, for instance, Cowley (2005).

25. It was also criticized as undermining the authority of Parliament.

26. Public Limited Company.

27. See the overall evaluation drawn up by the *Financial Times*: "Brown's Bequest: The British Treasury Contemplates the Waning of Its Power," 22 March 2007: 11.

Chapter 4

1. An analysis defended, in particular, by a flagship magazine of the 1980s, *Marxism Today*, which was edited by Martin Jacques and featured, among others, Stuart Hall, Charles Leadbeater, and Geoff Mulgan. The last two became influential advisors to Blair.

2. Clause 4 of the 1918 constitution was printed on the back of membership cards. It spelled out the aims and values of the party, such as the nationalization of industries and services. Several attempts to amend it failed before Tony Blair took up the challenge in his first speech as leader in September 1994.

3. Proclamation by Tony Blair on the day of his election, 2 May 1997.

4. Local government is a traditional reservoir of politicians and activists for the Labour Party. The 1997 general election victory had been preceded by steady local gains through the 1990s. Since 2000, Labour has regularly lost seats as well as overall control of local councils. See the discussion of local politics as incentive for participation in Whiteley and Seyd (2002: 101–2).

5. According to Peter Mair, one of the objectives of the New Labour elites was precisely to empty the party of its substance. See Mair (2000).

6. See the fine and comprehensive book by Lewis Minkin on trade unions and their difficult relationships with Labour (1992).

7. Unprecedentedly for a movement rather hostile to Europe, John Monks invited Jacques Delors, then president of the European Commission, to a TUC

congress. Monks is today president of the European Trade Union Confederation (ETUC).

8. This occurred in 1995. See below.

9. Notably during the choice of a candidate for mayor of London, or for the leadership of the party in Wales.

10. The so-called One Member, One Vote policy yielded the decidedly elegant acronym OMOV.

11. The vote concerned pension reform, which was opposed by the unions.

12. For example, 27 percent of the membership took part in the key 1995 vote on clause 4, and 25 percent in the internal elections for the National Executive Committee in 2000. See Faucher-King (2005): 207–8.

13. As late as 2003, the BBC offered nearly eleven hours of live programs on television for each of the three major party conferences.

14. See the report by the Neill Committee (1998: 40). They remain important financial contributors: between 1997 and 2006, union leaders contributed more than £100 million to the Labour Party's finances.

15. In 1998 the party's expenditure rose to more than £20 million, far exceeding the declared reserves of £12 million.

16. See the fascinating analysis of the 2004 Democratic presidential campaign by Dana Fisher (2006).

17. Among the donors was Bernie Ecclestone, an important player in Formula One racing, who obtained an exemption from the ban on tobacco advertising in the sport imposed by the European Union and David (now Lord) Salisbury, a minister but also the owner and director of the supermarket chain of the same name.

18. Particularly in the context of private clubs of benefactors.

19. On the contrary, it was firms that were disturbed by the reaction of their shareholders to their close association with political parties.

20. The Conservatives borrowed more than £35 million on the same terms.

21. The "sale" of titles has been illegal since 1925.

22. The last years of the Conservative regime had been marked by a proliferation of scandals and accusations of corruption. The Blair governments were not spared: ministers resigned for having obtained financial loans under dubious circumstances; the party paid back suspect loans; and the government was suspected of having abused the Honours List.

23. See the pioneering work on political marketing by Jennifer Lees-Marshment (2001) and Wring (2005). See also Faucher-King (2009).

24. The at least symbolic preservation of conference sovereignty was a sine qua non of acceptance of the reforms by activists (in particular, the delegates charged with adopting the constitutional reforms).

25. The 1992 defeat is often attributed to the bitter hostility of the populist press toward Kinnock's party.

26. Alastair Campbell, the prime minister's press spokesman until 2003, was regarded as one of the most powerful nonelected politicians by virtue of his influence on the prime minister's strategic, political, and communications choices. His closeness to Tony Blair and his official role made him the privileged interlocutor, feared and detested, of many journalists.

27. Alastair Campbell, evidence to House of Commons Select Committee on Public Administration, June 1998 (available on the Internet site http://www.publications.parliament.uk/pa/cm199798/cmselect/cmpubadm/770/8062307.htm).

28. In 1997 Tony Blair himself went to meet the press magnate Rupert Murdoch and secured the support of his main newspapers, including the *Sun*.

29. From 1996 the computer program *Excalibur* made it possible to rapidly track down Conservative arguments and quotations, in order to counter their media impact and expose contradictions and shifts in position. The party's communications were articulated around three Rs: rhetoric, repetition, and rebuttal.

30. See, for instance, BBC journalist Nick Jones's criticism (1999).

Chapter 5

1. See the Internet site http://www.open.ac.uk/.

2. The British are subjects of the Crown. The vocabulary of citizenship is recent in Britain, on account of a strong conception of representative democracy and popular sovereignty, and because of the conviction that popular participation is not in itself positive, whereas delegation is a criterion of civic culture.

3. See the analysis of British Labour and socialist currents in the reference book by Samuel H. Beer (1982).

4. See the Internet site http://www.psa.ac.uk/.

5. Tony Blair, speech to the World Economic Forum, Davos, 27 January 2005.

6. The influence of Adam Smith and economic liberalism is clear here. See Hay (2007): 57.

7. Unlike immigrants from the Caribbean, Muslim immigrants in the United Kingdom have tended to develop in isolation from other communities. The engagement in Iraq marked the beginning of a marked increase in abstentions in Labour constituencies with high Muslim populations. See Joly (1995).

8. See the sharp analysis developed by Jordan and Maloney (2007).

9. *The Times*, 21 December 2004.

10. The British have invented the term "chuggers" (charity muggers).

11. Constant and sometimes tiresome. . . . To avoid this trap, canvassing by subcontracting organizations was increasingly used during the 1990s. The sharing and even the purchase of mailing lists makes it possible to select potential benefactors very carefully (according to their consumer profile). Britain has developed a highly advanced technology for sorting according to the profile of consumers of different services and products, but has few safeguards concerning the use of such information. See Jordan and Maloney (2007).

12. According to Benedict Anderson (1983), imagined communities are virtual in that their members will never all be able to meet and therefore have to imagine their common destiny.

13. See the hard-hitting analysis by Skocpol (2002).

14. See the Internet site, http://www.ramblers.org.uk/supportus/.

15. They now supply services in exchange for membership: subscriptions, legal aid, and the like.

16. See the article by Kendall and Knapp (2000, available on the Internet at http://www.lse.ac.uk).

17. The British have been struck by a series of health crises in the area of food, in particular the contamination of eggs by salmonella in the 1980s and then the epidemic of bovine spongiform encephalopathy ("mad cow disease") in the 1990s.

18. This is doubtless one of the most important innovative aspects of New Labour, which distanced itself from a Labour tradition strongly marked by working-class culture and domestic paternalism. It is sometimes difficult to understand the violence of press attacks over these issues (one thinks of the *Sun* headline comparing the government to a "Gay Mafia").

19. Labour first took control of its media strategy during the years of Opposition (Stanyer 2001) and used its new expertise at handling the news while in power to promote both the party and the government.

20. See the enlightening work by Caroline Lee (2008) on the professionalization and the commodification of deliberative democratic procedures. Also Atkinson (1999) and Barnes (2007).

21. Youtube is a site for sharing videos: http://www.youtube.com.

22. Ros Taylor, "E-government Fails to Catch On," *The Guardian*, 15 December 2003.

23. "Your care, your health, your say" consulted nearly forty-three thousand people, about a quarter of them through a "National Citizens' Summit" held in Birmingham on 29 October 2005 or through local forums.

24. Public consultation exercises seem particularly effective for assessing which public expense can be disposed of with the least protest, as the consultation process usually starts from the "common sense" assumption that a cut is inevitable. Similarly, they rarely challenge existing social hierarchies. See Barnes (2007).

25. The disclaimers of Conservative governments in the "mad cow" crisis alerted British people to the ambiguous relations between science and political power, particularly as a result of "closed communities" in policy-formation procedures for agriculture and food. In 1999 the polling institute MORI revealed that 73 percent of British people rejected GMO agriculture and 60 percent also doubted its safety. In 2003, the Food Standards Agency used a citizens' jury to demonstrate how an informed public would welcome the availability of GM food in the UK. The full report can be found at http://www.food.gov.uk/gmdebate/citizens_jury/?view=GM%20Microsite.

26. This was a residential tax per capita (and hence not proportional to living space) introduced by the Thatcher government in 1990.

27. The role of the chief whip is to ensure that MPs are present during votes and follow party instructions.

28. *The Guardian*, 29 December 2006.

29. Mobilizations against the war in Iraq also involved Labour MPs. There were 11 rebels against the intervention in Afghanistan in November 2001, 53 during the first vote on intervention in Iraq in September 2002, and 132 during the fifth and last vote on the issue on 18 March 2003.

30. To attract media attention is not only a success in itself but also a way of popularizing a cause. Thus an association of divorced fathers (Fathers 4 Justice) made themselves famous for their media coups in foiling security measures (particularly those at Buckingham Palace).

31. This amendment to the law on local government, introduced in 1988, prohibited the "promotion" of homosexuality in schools. It was sometimes interpreted as a ban on any mention of homosexuality. It was repealed in 2003.

32. Having emerged in 1992 in the United Kingdom, Earth First played an important role in the development of such tactics and, in particular, contributed to celebrated mobilizations at Twyford Downs and Newbury between 1992 and 1997. It involves a loose coordination of occasional, informal cells. More recently, Reclaim the Street has adopted the same tactics. Doherty et al. (2003).

33. Alternative movements have used their own media since the 1990s and, in particular, produce their own films and documentaries. They have also invaded the Internet as a tool of internal and external communication.

34. He had had published an anti-Labour campaign poster showing a policeman with one hand tied behind his back under the slogan "Labour's Soft on Crime." In 2002, Teresa May, then chairman of the party, chastised the Conservative conference to change its practices and demonstrate that they were no longer the "nasty party."

35. *The Big Issue*, 6–12 January 1997. See also Dean (1999: 14).

36. Randall (2004). For a ferocious and brilliantly written critique, see the work of the *Observer* journalist Nick Cohen (2003).

37. The Anti-Terrorism, Crime and Security Act (2001), the Prevention of Terrorism Act (2005), and the Terrorism Act (2006).

38. The principle of indefinite detention is incompatible with both the European Convention and the British tradition of civil liberties.

39. This is all the more problematic inasmuch as a number of memory sticks, data CDs, and computer hard drives containing highly sensitive and confidential information (for instance, details of bank accounts or history of incarceration or even antiterrorism files from MI5) have been lost or stolen in recent years as a result of negligence by either governmental employees or employees of contracted companies.

40. A young woman, Maya Evans, was arrested and convicted in October

2005 for having rung a bell in front of Parliament and read out the names of British soldiers killed in Iraq.

41. Parliament eventually raised the number of days of detention without charge for suspected terrorists to forty-two days in 2008.

42. Some services have been transformed into agencies (probation service), specializing in very specific tasks: rationalization of resources, financial autonomy, performance-related pay, widespread adoption of new methods for producing and tracking information on cases, districts, or individuals.

43. According to the catch-phrase of George Orwell's cult novel of 1948, *1984*.

44. Report of the Privacy International association, available on the Internet site http://www.privacyinternational.org.

45. The home secretary also justified this program in terms of prevention: removing problem individuals from their gang would reduce the risks of antisocial behavior or recidivism.

Conclusion

1. More prudent, the Conservatives prefer to stress the right to govern conferred by electoral victory. See Faucher-King (2003).

Postscript

1. See www.hmtreasury.gov.uk/barker_review_of_housing_supply_recommendations.htm.

2. The report was published by a respected economist and advisor to Tony Blair, Lord Stern. The conclusion was to underline that early action on climate change would outweigh its costs. In 2008, Lord Stern revised its suggestion to take into account the acceleration of CO_2 releases. See www.occ.gov.uk/activities/stern.htm.

3. The fees, however, are applied to British students who are not normally resident in Scotland.

4. The Scottish Green Party (an organization independent from its sister UK party) has sent representatives to Holyrood since 1999. Although the number of MSPs was reduced to two in 2007, it has retained a voice on the national political scene.

5. See Chapter 1.

6. See http://www.youtube.com/watch?v=7iPaiylUYW0.

7. His resignation from the cabinet in May 2009 was perceived as an important blow to Gordon Brown, as it gave credibility to the brewing rebellion among Labour ranks.

8. Nine ministers and secretaries of state resigned during this period.

Bibliography

Almond, Gabriel, and Sydney Verba. 1963. *Civic Culture*. Boston: The Little Brown Series in Comparative Politics.

Anderson, Benedict. 1983. *Imagined Communities: Reflections on the Origin and Spread of Nationalism*. London: Verso.

Anderson, Jenny. 2007. "Socializing Capital, Capitalizing the Social: Contemporary Social Democracy and the Knowledge Economy." *Center for European Studies Working Paper series*, 145, Harvard University.

Annesley, Clare, and Andrew Gamble. 2004. "Economic and Welfare Policy," in Steve Ludlam and Martin J. Smith (eds.), *Governing as New Labour: Policy and Politics under Blair*. Basingstoke: Palgrave, pp. 144–60.

Armstrong, Hilary. 2000. "The Invisible Generation: From Picking Up the Pieces to Predicting and Preventing." Sunderland. Speech at the Institute of Public Policy Research, 20 May.

Atkinson, Anthony B., and Thomas Piketty (eds.). 2007. *Top Incomes over the Twentieth Century: A Contrast between European and English-speaking Countries*. Oxford: Oxford University Press.

Atkinson, Rob. 1999. "Discourses of Partnership and Empowerment in Contemporary British Urban Regeneration." *Urban Studies* 36: 59–72.

Auclair, Philippe. 2007. *Le Royaume enchanté de Tony Blair*. Paris: Fayard.

Baker, David, and David Seawright. 1998. "A Rosy Map of Europe? Labour Parliamentarians and European Integration," in David Baker and David Seawright (eds.), *Britain For and Against Europe: British Politics and the Question of European Integration*. Oxford: Oxford University Press, pp. 57–87.

Barnes, Marian. 2007. "Whose Spaces? Contestations and Negotiations in

Health and Regeneration Forums in England," in A. Cornwell and V. Schattan Coelho (eds.), *Spaces for Change*. London: Zed Books.

Beer, Samuel H. 1982. *Modern British Politics*. London: Faber and Faber.

Bennie, Lynn, and Alistair Clark. 2003. "Towards Moderate Pluralism: Scotland's Post-Devolution Party System 1999–2002." *British Elections and Parties Review* 13: 134–55.

Bevir, Mark. 2005. *New Labour: A Critique*. London: Routledge.

Blair, Tony. 1996. *New Britain: My Vision of a Young Country*. London: Fourth Estate.

———. 2004. "Labour Conference: Leader's Speech," http://news.bbc.co.uk/2/hi/uk_news/politics/3697434.stm.

Bogdanor, Vernon (ed.). 2005. *Joined-up Government*. Oxford: Oxford University Press.

Boyce, Robert. 2005. "Grande-Bretagne/Etats-Unis: une relation speciale a sens unique?" in Jacques Leruez (ed.), *Londres et le Monde: Stratèges et stratégies britanniques*. Paris: CERI Autrement, pp. 39–80.

Bulmer, Simon, and Martin Burch. 2006. "Central Government," in Ian Bache and Andrew Jordan (eds.), *The Europeanization of British Politics*. Basingstoke: Palgrave, pp. 37–51.

Burnham, Peter. 2001. "New Labour and the Politics of Depoliticisation." *British Journal of Politics and International Relations* 3(2): 127–49.

Carnie, Fiona. 2003. *Alternative Approaches to Education: A Guide for Parents and Teachers*. London: Routledge.

Cassis, Youssef. 1987. *Le City de Londres 1870–1914*. Paris: Belin.

Chapman, Rachael. 2005. "The Third Sector," in Ian Bache and Andrew Jordan (eds.), *The Europeanization of British Politics*. Houndsmill: Palgrave, pp. 168–83.

Clarke, John. 2004. "Creating Citizen-Consumers: The Trajectory of an Identity." Canadian Anthropological Society Conference, University of Western Ontario, May.

Clift, Ben, and Jim Tomlinson. 2007. "Complexity, Constraint and New Labour's Putative Neo-liberalism: A Reply to Colin Hay." *British Journal of Political Science* 37(2): 378–81.

Cohen, Nick. 2003. *Pretty Straight Guys*. London: Faber and Faber.

Cowley, Philip. 2002. *Revolts and Rebellions: Parliamentary Voting under Blair*. London: Politico's.

———. 2005. *Rebels: How Blair Mislaid His Majority*. London: Politico's.

Crewe, Emma. 2005. *Lords of Parliament: Manners, Rituals and Politics*. Manchester: Manchester University Press.

Crouch, Colin. 2004. *Post Democracy*. Oxford: Blackwell.

———. 2008. "What Will Follow the Demise of Private Keynesianism?" *Political Quarterly* 79(4): 476–87.

Crowley, John. 1999. *Sous les épines, la rose*. Paris: La Découverte.

Danchev, Alex. 2007. "Tony Blair's Vietnam: The Iraq War and the 'Special Relationship' in Historical Perspective." *Review of International Studies* 33: 189–203.

Dean, Hartley (ed.). 1999. *Begging Questions: Street-level Economic Activity and Social Policy Failure*. Bristol: Policy Press.

Doherty, Brian, Alexandra Plows, and Derek Wall. 2003. "'The Preferred Way of Doing Things': The British Direct Action Movement." *Parliamentary Affairs* 56(4): 669–86.

Doherty, Brian, Matthew Paterson, and Benjamin Seel (eds.). 2000. *Direct Action in British Environmentalism*. London: Routledge.

Driver, Stephen. 2006. "Modernizing the Public Services," in Patrick Dunleavy, Richard Heffernan, Philip Cowley, and Colin Hay (eds.), *Developments in British Politics 8*. Basingstoke: Palgrave, pp. 272–94.

Drucker, Henry. 1979. *Doctrine and Ethos in the Labour Party*. London: Allen and Unwin.

Dunleavy, Patrick. 2006. "The Westminster Model and the Distinctiveness of British Politics," in Patrick Dunleavy et al. (eds.), *Developments in British Politics 8*. Basingstoke: Palgrave, pp. 315–40.

Farrell, David, and Paul Webb. 2000. "Political Parties as Campaign Organizations," in Russell Dalton and Martin Wattenberg (eds.), *Parties without Partisans: Political Change in Advanced Industrial Democracies*. Oxford : Oxford University Press, pp. 102–28.

Faucher, Florence. 2000. "Le système électoral britannique," in Pascal Delwitt and Jean-Michel De Waele (eds.), *Le mode de scrutin fait-il l'élection?* Bruxelles: Editions de l'université de Bruxelles, pp. 51–71.

Faucher-King, Florence. 2003. "Brève passion ou engagement durable? La démocratie interne et le parti conservateur britannique," in Pascal Perrineau (ed.), *La démocratie en mouvement*. Paris: Editions de l'Aube, pp. 149–74.

———. 2005. *Changing Parties: An Anthropology of British Political Party Conferences*. Basingstoke: Palgrave.

———. 2009. "The Party Is Over: The 'Modernization' of the British Labour

Party," in Terrence Casey (ed.), *Britain after Blair*. Basingstoke: Palgrave, pp. 39–51.

Finlayson, Alan. 2003. *Making Sense of New Labour*. London: Lawrence and Wishart.

Fisher, Dana. 2006. *Activism, Inc. How the Outsourcing of Grassroots Campaigns Is Strangling Progressive Politics in America*. Stanford: Stanford University Press.

Flinders, Mathew. 2006. "The Half Hearted Constitutional Revolution," in Patrick Dunleavy et al. (eds.), *Developments in British Politics 8*, pp. 117–37.

Foley, Mikael 2004. "Presidential Attribution as an Agency of Prime Ministerial Critique in a Parliamentary Democracy: The Case of Tony Blair." *British Journal of Politics and International Relations*, 6(3): 292–311.

Fondation Robert-Schuman. 2006. "Productivité, temps de travail and taux d'emploi dans l'Union européenne," *Questions d'Europe* 45(20) (November). http://www.robert-schuman.org/archives_questions_europe.php.

Freedland, M. R. 2001. "The Marketization of Public Services," in C. Crouch, K. Eder, and D. Tambini (eds.), *Citizenship, Markets and the State*. Oxford: Clarendon Press.

Gamble, Andrew. 1988. *The Strong State and the Free Economy*. Basingstoke: Palgrave.

———. 2004. *Between Europe and America: The Future of British Politics*. Basingstoke: Palgrave.

———. 2007. "New Labour and Old Debates," in Gerry Hassan (ed.), *After Blair: Politics after the New Labour Decade*. London: Lawrence and Wishart, pp. 20–35.

Gauja, Anika. 2009. " Moving Beyond the Membership? The Transformation of Party Organisations, Policy Outsourcing and the Creation of Supporters' Networks." American Political Science Association Congress, Toronto.

Glyn, Andrew, and Stewart Wood. 2003. "New Labour's Economic Policy," in Andrew Glyn (ed.), *Social Democracy in Neoliberal Times: The Left and Economic Policy since 1980*. Oxford: Oxford University Press, pp. 200–22.

Greer, Scott L. 2006. "The Fragile Divergence Machine: Citizenship, Policy Divergence and Devolution," in Alan Trench (ed.), *Devolution and Power*. Manchester: Manchester University Press.

Hale, Sara. 2006. *Blair's Community: Communitarian Thought and New Labour*. Manchester: Manchester University Press.

Harris, Phil. 2002. "Strategic Corporate Lobbying: The Evolution of Strategic

Political Lobbying in the UK and the Psychological Network Underpinning Machiavellian Marketing." *Journal of Political Marketing* 1(1): 237–49.

Hassan, Gerry (ed.). 2007. *After Blair: Politics after the New Labour Decade*. London: Lawrence and Wishart.

Hay, Colin. 1999. *The Political Economy of New Labour*. Manchester: Manchester University Press.

———. 2007. "What's in a Name? New Labour's Putative Keynesianism." *British Journal of Political Science* 37(1): 187–92.

Heath, Anthony, Roger Jowell, and John Curtice. 2001. *The Rise of New Labour*. Oxford: Oxford University Press.

Heffernan, Richard. 2003. "Prime Ministerial Predominance? Core Executive Politics in the UK." *British Journal of Politics and International Relations* 5(3): 347–72.

Heffernan, Richard, and Paul Webb. 2005. "The British Prime Minister: Much More than 'First among Equals,'" in Thomas Poguntke and Paul Webb (eds.), *The Presidentialization of Politics—A Comparative Study of Modern Democracies*. Oxford: Oxford University Press.

Hindmoor, Andrew. 2004. *New Labour at the Centre: Constructing Political Space*. Oxford: Oxford University Press.

Hood, Christopher. 2006. "Gaming in Targetworld: The Target Approach to Managing British Public Services." *Public Administration Review* 66(4): 515–21.

Hood, Christopher, Colin Scott, Oliver James, George Jones, and Tony Travers. 1999. *Regulation inside Government: Waste Watchers, Quality Police and Sleaze Busters*. Oxford: Oxford University Press.

Jeffrey, Charlie, and Daniel Wincott. 2006. "Devolution in the UK: Statehood and Citizenship in Transition." *Publius* 36(1): 3–18.

Jenkins, Simon. 1996. *Accountable to None: Tory Nationalization of Britain*. London: Penguin.

Johnson, Neville. 2004. *Reshaping the British Constitution*. Basingstoke: Palgrave.

Joly, Danièle. 1995. *Britannia's Crescent: Making a Place for Muslims in British Society*. Aldershot: Avebury.

Jones, Barry, and Michael Keating. 1985. *Labour and the British State*. Oxford: Clarendon Press.

Jones, Nicholas. 1999. *Sultans of Spin*. London: Orion.

Jordan, Grant, and William A. Maloney. 2007. *Democracy and Interest Groups*. Basingstoke: Palgrave.

Jowell, Roger, John Curtice, and Anthony Heath. 1994. *Labour's Last Chance? The 1992 Election and Beyond*. Dartmouth: Ashgate.

Keating, Michael. 2005. *The Government of Scotland: Public Policy after Devolution*. Edinburgh: Edinburgh University Press.

Keegan, William. 2004. *The Prudence of Mr Gordon Brown*. Chichester: John Wiley and Sons.

Kendall, Jeremy, and Martin Knapp. 2000. "The Third Sector and Welfare State Modernization: Inputs, Activities and Comparative Performance." *Civil Society Working Paper*, no. 14. http://wwww.lse.ac.uk/collections/CCS/publications/cswp/civil_society_wp.htm

King, Desmond. 1999. *In the Name of Liberalism: Illiberal Social Policy in Britain and the United States*. Oxford: Oxford University Press.

Lascoumes, Pierre, and Patrick Le Galès (eds.). 2004. *Gouverner par les instruments*. Paris: Presses de Sciences Po.

Le Galès, Patrick. 2004. "Contrôle et surveillance, la restructuration de l'État en Grande-Bretagne," in Lascoumes Pierre and Patrick Le Galès (eds.), *Gouverner par les instruments*. Paris: Presses de Sciences Po, pp. 237–72.

———. 2006. "Gouvernance," in Laure Boussaguet, Sophie Jacquot, and Pauline Revinet (eds.), *Dictionnaire des politiques publiques*. Paris: Presses de Sciences Po.

Le Galès, Patrick, and Alan Scott. 2008. "Une révolution bureaucratique britannique? Autonomie sans contrôle ou *freer markets, more rules.*" *Revue française de sociologie* 49(2): 301–30.

Lee, Caroline. 2008. "Consuming Democracy, Democratizing Consumption." American Political Science Association Congress. Boston.

Lees-Marshment, Jennifer. 2001. *Political Marketing and British Political Parties: The Party's Just Begun*. Manchester: Manchester University Press.

Leruez, Jacques. 1983. *L'Écosse, une nation sans État*. Lille: Presses Universitaires de Lille.

———. 2005. "Vers une Europe Anglo-Saxonne," in Jacques Leruez (ed.), *Londres et le Monde: Stratèges et statégies britanniques*. Paris: CERI Autrement, pp. 81–111.

Lewis, Jane. 2003. "What Is New Labour? Can It Deliver on Social Policies?" in Jane Lewis and Rebecca Surrender (eds.), *Welfare State Change: Towards a Third Way?* Oxford: Oxford University Press.

Ludlam, Steve, and Martin J. Smith (eds.). *Governing as New Labour: Policy and Politics under Blair*. Basingstoke: Palgrave.

Lusoli, Wainer, Stephen Ward, and Rachel Gibson. 2006. "(Re)connecting Politics? Parliament, the Public and the Internet." *Parliamentary Affairs* 59(1): 24–42.

Mair, Peter. 2000. "Partyless Democracy: Solving the Paradox of New Labour?" *New Left Review* 2(2): 21–35.

Mandelson, Peter, and Roger Liddle. 1998. *The Blair Revolution: Can New Labour Deliver?* London: Faber and Faber.

Massey, Andrew. 1999. *The State of Britain: A Guide to the UK Public Sector.* London: Public Management and Policy Association.

Massey, Andrew, and Robert Piper. 2005. *Public Management and Modernisation in Britain.* Basingstoke: Palgrave.

Meyer, John, and Brian Rowan. 1977. "Institutionalized Organizations: Formal Structure as Myth and Ceremony." *American Journal of Sociology* 83(2): 340–63.

Micheletti, Michele. 2003. *Political Virtue and Shopping: Individuals, Consumerism, and Collective Action.* New York: Palgrave.

Miller, David, and William Dinan. 2000. "The Rise of the PR Industry in Britain, 1979–98." *European Journal of Communication* 15(1): 5–35.

Minkin, Lewis. 1992. *The Contentious Alliance: Trade Unions and the Labour Party.* Edinburgh: Edinburgh University Press.

Mitchell, James. 2006. "Unity of Government, Political Equality and Diverse Institutions: The UK Territorial Constitution in Historic Perspective," in A. Trench (ed.), *Devolution and Power in the UK State.* Manchester: Manchester University Press.

Moran, Michael. 2003. *The British Regulatory State: High Modernism and Hyper Innovation.* Oxford: Oxford University Press.

Neill, Lord. 1998. *Report of the Committee on Standards in Public Life on the Finding of Political Parties in the UK.* Vol. 1, CM4057–1. London: Stationery Office.

Nick, Randall. 2004. "Three Faces of New Labour: Principle, Pragmatism and Populism in New Labour's Home Office," in Steve Ludlam and Martin J. Smith (eds.), *Governing as New Labour: Policy and Politics under Blair.* Basingstoke: Palgrave, pp. 177–92.

Norton, Philip. 2005. *Parliament in British Politics.* Basingstoke: Palgrave.

Opinion Leader Research. 2006. "Your Health, Your Care, Your Say—Research Report." Online publication: http://www.dh.gov.uk/en/Publicationsandstatistics/Publications/PublicationsPolicyAndGuidance/DH_4127357.

Paterson, Lindsay, Alice Brown, John Curtis, and Kerstin Hinds. 2001. *New Scotland, New Politics?* Edinburgh: Edinburgh University Press.

Pattie, Charles, Patrick Seyd, and Paul Whiteley. 2003. "Civic Attitudes and Engagement in Modern Britain." *Parliamentary Affairs* 56(4): 616–33.

———. 2004. *Citizenship in Britain: Values, Participation and Democracy.* Cambridge: Cambridge University Press.

Plant, Raymond, Mark Beech, and Hickson Keith (eds.). 2004. *The Struggle for Labour's Soul.* London: Routledge.

Polanyi, Karl. 1957. *The Great Transformation: The Political and Economic Origins of Our Time.* London: Beacon Press.

Pollard, Naomi, Maria Latorre, and Dhananjayan Sriskandarajah. 2008. "Floodgates or Turnstiles? Post EU-Enlargement Migration Flows to (and from) the EU." IPPR, http://www.ippr.org.uk/publicationsandreports/publication.asp?id=603.

Pollitt, Christopher, Colin Talbot, Janice Caulfield, and Amada Smullen. 2004. *Agencies: How Governments Do Things through Semi-autonomous Organisations.* Basingstoke: Palgrave.

Power, Michael. 1997. *The Audit Society: Rituals of Verification.* Oxford: Oxford University Press.

Rawnsley, Andrew. 2001. *Servants of the People.* London: Penguin Books.

Richards, David, and Martin J. Smith. 2004. "The Hybrid State: New Labour's Response to the Challenge of Governance," in Steve Ludlam and Martin J. Smith (eds.), *Governing as New Labour: Policy and Politics under Blair.* Basingstoke: Palgrave pp. 106–26.

Rod, Rhodes. 1996. *Understanding Governance.* London: Palgrave.

Routledge, Paul. 1999. *Mandy: The Unauthorised Biography of Peter Mandelson.* London: Routledge.

Russell, Meg. 2000. *Reforming the House of Lords: Lessons from Overseas.* Oxford University Press.

———. 2005. *Building New Labour: The Politics of Party Organisation.* Basingstoke: Palgrave.

Saint Martin, Denis. 2001. *Building the Managerialist State.* Oxford: Oxford University Press.

Sanders, David, Harold Clarke, Marianne Stewart, and Paul Whiteley. 2003. "The Dynamics of Protest in Britain, 2000–2002." *Parliamentary Affairs* 56(4): 687–99.

Seldon, Anthony. 2004. *Blair: The Biography.* London: Free Press.

Seyd, Patrick, and Paul Whiteley. 1992. *Labour's Grass Roots: The Politics of Party Membership*. Oxford: Clarendon Press.

———. 2002. *New Labour's Grassroots: The Transformation of the Labour Party Membership*. Basingstoke: Palgrave.

Shaw, Eric. 1993. "Towards Renewal? The British Labour Party's Policy Review." *West European Politics* 16(1): 112–32.

Sklair, Leslie. 2001. *The Transnational Capitalist Class*. Oxford: Blackwell.

Skocpol, Theda. 2002. "United States: From Membership to Advocacy," in Robert D. Putnam (ed.), *Democracies in Flux: The Evolution of Social Capital in Contemporary Society*. Oxford: Oxford University Press, pp. 103–36.

Stanyer, James. 2001. *The Creation of Political News: Television and British Party Political Conferences*. Brighton: Sussex Academic Press.

Stoker, Gerry. 2004. *Transforming Local Governance: From Thatcherism to New Labour*. Basingstoke: Palgrave.

Taylor, Robert. 2005. "Mr Blair's British Business Model: Capital and Labour in Flexible Markets," in Seldon Anthony and Dennis Kavannagh (eds.), *The Blair Effect 2001–2005*. Cambridge: Cambridge University Press, pp. 184–206.

Toynbee, Polly, and David Walker. 2005. *Better or Worse? Has Labour Delivered?* London: Bloomsbury.

Webb, Paul. 2000. "Political Parties: Adapting to the Electoral Market," in Patrick Dunleavy, Andrew Gamble, Ian Holliday, and Gillian Peele (eds.), *Developments in British Politics 6*. Basingstoke: Palgrave, pp. 151–68.

Weir, Stuart, and David Beetham. 1999. *Political Power and Democratic Control in Britain*. London: Routledge.

Whiteley, Paul F., and Patrick Seyd. 2002. *High Intensity Participation: The Dynamics of Party Activism in Britain*. Ann Arbor: University of Michigan Press.

Wring, Dominic. 2005. *The Politics of Marketing the Labour Party*. Basingstoke: Palgrave.